A Journey To HELL and Back

The Flip Side

Charlotte Russell Johnson

with

Henry Johnson

These Cycles

Oh God, these cycles when will they end...
Whenever I look around...
There they go again...
Dear God, these cycles where did they begin...

Oh God, these cycles please let them end...
My will can't You bend...
It's no longer re-peat, three-peat, or four-peat...
My crimes continue to compete...

Oh God, these cycles when will they end...
It's a battle some say that we can't win...
But God, You were with me when they began...
For victory, on You I depend...

Oh God, it began as a nag...
This opened the hole in the bag...
The nag was the only weapon I had...
Before I knew it I was mad...

Oh God, these cycles were disguised as my friends...
They were really hidden sin...
It was trying to destroy me from within...
Dear God, I know you are my true friend...

Oh God, these cycles seek to destroy your plan...
But God, You created man...
My heart is in Your hand...
Through this pain make me a witness to man...

My God, these cycles are with me wherever I turn ...
Help me this lesson to learn...
These cycles are out of hand...
Make them cease at Your command...

Dear God, make me putty in Your hands...
Make Your wishes my command...
It's on You that I depend...
You have been my closest friend...

Oh God, these cycles must cease...
Please help me to hold my peace...
That I might glorify Thee...
Let it be only You that they see...

Dear God, glorify your name...
Let this be the new game...
These cycles can't last...
You are the first and the last...

Dear God, help me to forget the past...
This pain is too great to last...
Help me through this some soul to win...
That in the end, You can call me friend...

Dear God, thank you so very much...
These cycles tried but my heart they couldn't touch...
For so long I've longed to be free...
You alone know what You created me to be...
I don't need to medicate...
Because my heart to You I dedicate...

Dedication

This book is dedicated to Earline and Herman Hall, the children who survived the cycles of madness. We are extremely proud of both of you.

In Memory
of
"The Champ"

Barbara Owens-Eberhart

11/24/1938-4/18/2002

For your devotion and obsession with my life, your belief in my God given potential, unselfish support, seeing me through the worse physical crisis in my life, sacrificing your own life, countless hours spent at Grady, making us laugh, you will never be forgotten.

INSIDE HELL

Preface

Recently, in what can only be termed an extreme leap of faith or an ultimate act of stupidity, I opened my life up to the public analysis of the world. After postponing writing *A Journey to Hell and Back* for a number of years, I began the agonizing process. It wasn't revisiting the events that caused my heart so much distress. Actually, the pain was caused by my professional experiences. As a professional, I have worked with numerous demographic groups classified as being at high risks for failure. Revealing the Good Samaritan had been a part of these populations caused me immense anguish. It never occurred to me that my new reputation was almost an idol god. Realizing I had a charge bigger than Charlotte, I defied my personal discomfort and wrote the book that today is bringing hope to so many people around the world.

A Journey to Hell and Back detailed major events in my life, which almost destroyed me, but instead served to make me a stronger person and a more effective lover of God. When I shared the manuscript with my husband, Henry, he said he needed to tell his side of the story. Originally, I didn't think seriously about the idea and almost resented the suggestion. However, after numerous requests for the sequel to my first book, I relented. *A Journey to Hell and Back: the Flip Side* will tell both sides of the journey. *The Flip Side* will be my husband's version of the event.

My second book, *Daddy's Hugs* exhorts the role of fatherhood in the lives of children. The book's major supposition is the role of fathers is essential to promote healthy child development and appropriate role modeling. *Daddy's Hugs* offers a striking commentary on the plight of fatherless children. Fathers are not depicted as merely financial breadwinners. They are portrayed as essential emotional caregivers. The book praises and provides examples of fathers who take an active role in parenting. There is an excellent balance of positive, negative, and neutral fathering role models. The book is able to stray away from the common mistake of male bashing. The devaluation of the role of fathers and their inadequate preparation for this role is explored in-depth. Women are not viewed as passive victims to be exploited by males, but as active participants in child rearing and parenting.

My books are written for those who need to know there is life after death; there is life after failure; there is life after sickness; there is life after divorce; and there is life after prison. The purpose in writing these books was not to glorify the failures or success in my life. The first book was written through my tears. The events contained within were all true. Sharing them was not meant to seek revenge or embarrass anyone. The events were only shared so those needing spiritual, emotional, and physical healing would be encouraged to seek life after hell. My books are continuing to fulfill their purpose.

Rather than cursing the darkness, I have chosen to light candles and thus begin to rise from the ashes of a life that literally burned itself out. This book will focus on two separate lives spiraling out of control that intersect on a road to destruction. It is often said two halves equal a whole. I beg to disagree. In marriage, two halves equal one fourth. When two broken or incomplete people unite in matrimony, chaos is inevitable. Rather than adding to each other, their competing needs are multiplied. Together, we are going to share the chaos resulting in our relationship. It is my desire that in sharing our separate struggles, which became a common struggle, others will be encouraged to hold on when all looks hopeless. Our lives can only be described as trips to the very pits of hell.

Nevertheless, beneath it all is a remarkable testimony of the love of God. This is not an attempt to glorify the devil or his angels, but to expose him as a thief and robber. He's still the accuser of the brethren and a destroyer of marriage and family.

Numerous people have commented, "You went through a lot." The operative word is through. I chose to go through the obstacles rather than succumbing to the forces trying to destroy me. It was also my choice not to drown in self-pity, revenge, or hatred. God alone has provided me the grace to forgive and maintain relationships with those who were instruments of destruction in my life. They were instruments or pawns in a plan bigger than their own.

My books are a testimony of the wonderful saving grace of my Lord and Savior, Jesus Christ, who loves us enough to even reach into the pits of hell and with the redemptive power of His blood snatch us back from hell's grip. Not only does He have this power, but He also has the power to work all things out for the good of those who love the Lord and who are the called according to His purpose.

I have offered my life as a source of hope and encouragement to every person looking for hope. It has often been remarked to me that I was courageous in opening my life up to others. There was no courage involved. It has been an act of total obedience to my Lord. I can never repay Him for all He has done for me. Perhaps in my obedience, I have shown a portion of my gratitude. My prayer is lives will be enriched by something written in these books.

The Flip Side

In any reporting of events, there are always several versions of the incidents: my side, your side, and the truth buried somewhere in the middle. In *A Journey to Hell and Back,* Charlotte told her side of the journey. In this book two sides will be told, her side and my side. Perhaps, the truth will come shining through in the end. Our lives often detour from their original course or destination. This book will share experiences anyone could have easily veered towards. Different circumstances and situations influence the success and failures in our lives. Failures are often inconvenient stumbling blocks. However, honest evaluation can turn obstacles of offence into stepping-stones.

The Bible teaches us to train up our children in the way they should go. It also assures us when the child is old (mature), he will not depart from it. This principle is true for everything we teach our children, whether good or evil. What we teach our children will become an inherent part of their lives.

The names of some individuals in this book have been changed to respect their rights to privacy. Other names have been changed to protect those who love them. Now, for those who enjoyed *A Journey to Hell and Back,* but had questions, we present to you, *A Journey to Hell and Back: The Flip Side.* We pray the unique format of this book will bless you.

All scripture references are from the King James Bible, unless otherwise noted.

_____Introduction by Earline Hall

A Journey to Hell and Back: The Flip Side is the third text in author Charlotte Russell Johnson's series of motivational books. Ms. Johnson true to form has developed a surprisingly unique book. The two major characters alternate narration of the story. This literary technique serves to mesmerize and hold the reader spellbound. Two separate individuals on parallel descents into hell collide violently, the force of which serves as a catalyst to accelerate their demise. Then just as all visible signs of hope evaporate, in a surprising plot twist surpassing Faulkner's As I Lay Dying, the text evolves into a completely different direction.

The Flip Side expands on Ms. Johnson's previous text, A Journey to Hell and Back, an autobiographical account of the author's life. The Flip Side further explores the author's life, while also giving the parallel and sometimes contrasting account of Ms. Johnson's husband, Henry. The text begins with the lives of two separate individuals in preparation for their first encounter and then chronicles their following union. This book is appealing to a wide and varied audience, including those preparing for marriage, divorce, raising a family, or a part of a family, involved in or getting out of a relationship, recovering from past mistakes, parenting, or in contact with any of these groups. This book humorously pokes fun at life's everyday problems. Mr. and Mrs. Johnson provide unique and sometimes competing perspectives of their life together. The text provides an insightfully honest portrait of the differing perspectives of a married couple. The varying interpretations of major events serve to keep the reader enchanted with the text. After reading this text the reader will wonder how often they have misunderstood the intention of others. The Johnson's invite you to decide what is the actual truth. They say there are two versions of every story and then there's the truth.

The Foundation Laid

But thou art He that took me out of the womb: Thou didst make me hope when I was upon my mother's breasts.
Psalm 22:9

On the cold winter night of February 3, 1959, Charlotte Anita Alexander was born. In the future, this name would become a source of contention for me. My grandmother had given birth to her youngest child, Carlton Earl Alexander two weeks earlier, January 14. Mama was downstairs in the living room when she realized something unusual was happening with her body. She made her way to the flight of steps leading to the upper level of the apartment. She was determined to make it to the top of the stairs to find an explanation for this change. On the upper level, there was a bathroom and three bedrooms. My grandmother, (Ma'Dear) was in the middle bedroom. After reaching the top of the stairs, Mama went into her mother's room. Once inside the room, she explained to her mother what was happening. Ma'Dear was familiar with the symptoms. She explained to her oldest daughter that she was in the early stages of the birthing process and needed to make appropriate preparations for the trip to the hospital.

Ma'Dear's youngest sister accompanied Mama to the hospital. Aunt Bobbie was Mama's aunt, but there was only eleven months difference in their ages. Aunt Bobbie was the oldest. She lived in the same housing project with her husband. At this time, Aunt Bobbie didn't have any children. She had already developed an attachment for the child my mother was carrying. This night would make the attachment worse. In the coming years, she would be overly concerned about everything I did. She would constantly remind me of one thing.

"You were supposed to be my baby."

She never forgot to tell me this and I never forgot I had another mother watching everything I did. Mama had promised to give me to Aunt Bobbie and her husband. After seeing me, Mama decided to keep her baby. During her pregnancy, Mama was overly embarrassed. As her pregnancy advanced, she had worn an over coat whenever she ventured outdoors. She was attempting to hide the growing bulge in her waste. At least, this is the way Aunt Bobbie told the story. She also remembered Mama crying out the night she was in labor.

"Lord, I want to run, but where can I hide?"

My father was stationed in Fort Bragg, North Carolina with the 82nd Airborne. He missed this momentous occasion, the birth of their first child. After my birth, we continued to reside with Mama's parents.

On Wednesday July 18, 1962, a decision was made that would dramatically affect my life for years to come. The circumstances surrounding the incident remain cloudy to me. The aftermath of this incident is very clear. The devastation resulting in my life is the clearest result.

Herman Russell, Jr. left a twenty-two-year-old widow and a three-year-old child to morn his passing. Mama was pregnant with their second child. My father was the second loss to our immediate family. My grandfather, Theodore Alexander, Sr. had passed when I was about a year old.

Be not far from me; for trouble is near; for there is none to help… Psalm 22:11

As Mama sat holding me on her lap at my father's funeral, she felt a shield of protection covering her. She knew God was protecting her and the unborn child she was carrying, the child her husband would never see. My grandfather had warned my mother, "If you look at a dead person, your baby will be born blind."

Mama didn't tell him, but inwardly, she had her own thoughts.

"I don't believe God would let my baby be born blind because I looked at her Daddy."

My sister, Crystal, arrived on schedule. She's never needed glasses. Ma'Dear said she was a screaming baby. This was attributed to the number of tears Mama shed during her pregnancy. After my father's death, we continued residing in Warren Williams Apartments. This is where most of the early years of my life were spent. It was my mother's choice to live in the projects. This housing project represented safety and security to her because she had spent most of her life there.

The first school I attended was Claflin Elementary. Carlton and I went to the same school. The school was several blocks away from the house. If we slowed around enough, it would be too late to walk. Mama would call her regular cab driver. On the days when we didn't have money to spend, we would tell him to pick us up from school. We didn't mind walking on the days when we had money to spend at a nearby store or gas station. Sometimes, Mama would send the cab driver to pick us up. We knew to check the front of the school for the cab before we began walking home.

There was another stop on our route home, Jill's Cafeteria. This was where Ma'Dear worked. Miss Jill owned the restaurant. She seemed like a nice lady. However, the restaurant was setup somewhat funny. We would go in the side door to see Ma'Dear. It was dimly lit and the furniture appeared worn. It was usually crowded. One day, I got a glimpse of another room in the restaurant. It was clean and well lighted. The furniture was in better condition. The next time we (Carlton and I) visited Jill's, we decided to come in through the other side. When we walked in, everybody stopped eating to stare at us. We didn't understand this. We proceeded to the counter to ask for Ma'Dear. We were taken to the back part of the restaurant. Ma'Dear told us to be sure to come through the side door next time. She never explained the reason for this stipulation. As I looked around, it finally dawned on me; all of the customers in the back room had one thing in common, the color of their skin. All of the customers in the front room had one thing in common, the color of their skin.

Carlton and I were always getting into something. Around the time we were five, a serious rainstorm came on suddenly. We were upstairs playing in one of the bedrooms. The window was open and began to swing on the hinges. Carlton reached his arm through the opening in the screen, attempting to close the window. He couldn't reach the window. I decided to try it. Determined not to be defeated, I stuck my head out the window. About this time, the wind shifted blowing the window towards me. In the end, the window collided with my forehead. Carlton began screaming at the top of his voice. When I pulled my head inside, there was blood dripping everywhere. He ran crying to the bathroom located next to the bedroom. When he returned, he was carrying a roll of toilet tissue. In an attempt to stop the flow of blood, he placed the roll of tissue on the gash in my forehead. This was our pattern of looking out for each other. Later, the wound was officially treated at the emergency room.

Carlton was my uncle, but we were also best friends. We did many things together. We began drinking and buying beer when we were around five years old. In the projects, there were several liquor houses. We knew the locations of these houses. We also knew which houses offered credit. One day, we decided we wanted a beer. We had been allowed to sip beer before. We told the woman who ran the house Ma'Dear wanted a beer on credit. She had an account with this lady. Ma'Dear soon found out what we had done, but we had already drunk the beer. Pickle (my mother's sister) and Ma'Dear thought it was funny. They didn't tell Mama.

There was a lady in Warren Williams who took us to church. We also attended Sunday school. This woman's husband didn't go to church with her. In following years, while she was at church, he tried to get me to come to their house. Mama didn't go to church either, but she sent us. When we were in the first or second grade we decided we wanted to join the church. We requested permission from our parents. The next Sunday, we were sprinkled. Our names were added to the church roll. We knew about Christ. Despite this knowledge, we didn't know Him.

Shortly thereafter, Mama moved her children away from Warren Williams for about three years. This was during my third through six grade years; however, my grandmother still resided in Warren Williams. Ma'Dear kept us most of the time when my mother was working. It was in Warren Williams where the foundation was laid for my journey to hell.

My mother felt the new neighborhood would be our salvation. It was supposed to be a better neighborhood. Mama was determined to give us the best of everything. We had steak dinners once a week. Everyone ate the steak of their choice. My favorite was T-bone. Crystal liked

New York Strips. On Wednesdays, we ate at Burger King, where we would often reorder several times. Sometimes, we ate two or three Whoppers each. We also enjoyed the barbecue from the Flamingo in East Wynnton. On Sunday, we usually cooked barbecue or chitterlings with all the trimmings. Mama worked at the Dixie Theatre, during this time period. On the nights when she was working, she would send a cab driver to bring us dinner. This was usually dinner from the Tally-Ho Grill. I loved their cornbread sticks. Sometimes when she returned home, she would bring us chicken or scrambled dogs from the Top Hat.

> *Now know I that the LORD saveth His anointed; He will hear him from His holy heaven with the saving strength of His right hand.* Psalm 20:6

During the years we were living away from Warren Williams, there were several attempted burglaries at our home. The last attempt was successful. This incident would leave my mother resolved to return to the safety of the project. After the burglary, Mama never slept sound again. In the middle of the night, I could hear her moving around the house. Often, she peeped out the windows, looking for a would-be intruder. If there was any sound outside the apartment, she heard it. Even cats covered by a veil of darkness were unable to escape her watchful eye. Although, she never said anything, I knew the burglar had left more than a scar across her arm.

The summer before I entered Junior High School, almost miraculously, the pounds began to drop off. By the time I began my seventh grade year, I was wearing a size nine. I had been a chubby child for years. My mother was excited about my going to Junior High School. For more than one reason, I merited a new wardrobe. Mama spared no expense in buying me new clothes and expensive shoes. Actually, I was no longer able to wear most of the clothes from the previous year. For years, my dresses had been wider than they were long. The dresses took on a new look; they were still wider than they were long, only for a different reason. Ma'Dear hemmed all my dresses and skirts for me. They had deep hems. The hems were too deep for Mama to master.

The mini dresses and mini skirts allowed me to show just the right amount of my legs. Maxi dresses were also in style. They were long dresses. I didn't own any of those. My attention was focused on making sure my legs looked good. I developed a love for cocoa butter. I was still very dissatisfied with my appearance. My memories of being fat were still vivid. Mama didn't like me to show my legs if there were scratches on them. This was part of her obsession with perfection.

The first time my ears were pierced, Mama was obsessed with the holes staying clean. Before I went to school each morning, she cleaned the sites several times. After a few days, the strings were removed from my ears, allowing the holes to close up. She also made sure no one ever saw ear wax in our ears.

"People look in your ears especially, when you go to the beauty shop."

No one ever saw my ears dirty. Before leaving the house each day, Mama took me to the back door. She would have me tilt my head towards the sun to give her a better view of my ear canal. The light in the house wasn't sufficient. She needed the help of the sun. Once when I was about nineteen, I was sitting in the swing on Ma'Dear's porch. Mama was sitting next me. Wouldn't you know it? She pulled my ear to get a better view and tried to clean it on the front porch! I reminded her, I was an adult. It wasn't appropriate for her to clean my ears in public. I still check my ears several times a day. I know she still looks in my ears.

Convinced my legs would have to be perfect, I began rubbing my legs with cocoa butter. It was supposed to remove any scars. That's what Mama told me. Whether this is true or not, I don't know. I didn't have any scars bigger than a pin scratch. My short dresses kept males of all ages looking and making passes at me. Lust had nothing to do with attractiveness. At the time, it didn't matter that they had only one interest. I had learned to accept this as one of the realities of life. They began sharing their financial resources with me. I knew they were hoping for something in return. This wasn't going to happen as long as they never caught me alone. Lustful hope would keep them giving their resources.

When I first began my new look, my great-great-grandmother expressed her concern over the length of my dresses. She was affectionately known by five generations of grandchildren as simply Mama. She was over a hundred years old and spent most of her time sitting in her rocking chair. Everybody in our family understood her. She stood her ground firmly. The walking cane by her side helped her to get her points across to us. No one talked back to her. She had earned her respect and place of authority in the family.

When my mother was a child, Mama had a special way to discipline the children. She would plat three pieces of thin tree branches together. Each of her braided switches had names. Dr. Butsey and Dr. A. helped to get her point across. At this point in her life, she was too old to manage this trick. Not to be out done by her age, she developed a new way to communicate her displeasure, the walking stick. Mama hooked me around the legs with her walking cane and pulled me towards her.

"Gal, where are you going with that shirt on?"

"Mama, this is a dress and this is the style."

I said it very softly and humbly. We knew we were never to disrespect her. I remained very still until she decided to release me. Afterwards, I changed the subject.

"Mama, what would you like to eat?"

Mama lived to be over a hundred years old. Some said she was a hundred and seven years old when she died. Others said a hundred and fourteen. She was born during slavery and I'm not sure of her exact age. God blessed her tremendously. She had a full head of long silver hair. It was as soft as a baby's hair. Her memory and health were in almost perfect condition until the end. During the last year of her life, she fell out of bed, breaking her hip. Her injury forced her to go to a nursing home to recover.

Before going to the nursing home, it was reported she took a "nip" occasionally. This was whenever she could get someone to slip it to her. It was commonly held that the nip helped her to live so long. Once in the nursing home, there no more slips of the nip. Mama died while recovering at the nursing home. Some people believed it was because she was no longer getting this occasional nip. In my young mind, I wondered why someone didn't slip it to her. After all, she never got drunk. No one would have been the wiser and Mama could have lived forever.

The seventh grade proved to be a turning point in my life. The trips home from school were often emotionally painful for me. On one of these trips home, someone explained to me that my mother and father weren't married when I was born. This new knowledge served as the catalyst that increased my detachment from my peers.

It not only broke my heart, shattering the one perfect thing in my life, my memory of my father, but also caused my mother's heart to be pierced with great sorrow for many years. This was when I learned about Mama wearing the coat during her pregnancy. I also learned why Aunt Bobbie insisted I was supposed to be her baby. Mama was embarrassed by her pregnancy.

I am weary with my groaning: all night I make
my bed to swim; I water my coach with tears.
Mine eyes are consumed because of grief; it
waxeth old because of mine enemies.
Psalm 6:6-7

In my deepest times of loneliness, I imagined what my life would be like if I had known my father. It never occurred to anyone, as time progressed, this incident would haunt me. After all, how do you explain death to a three-year-old? This over site would cause many years of grief in our family. It was during this period the absence of my father began to weigh heaviest on my mind. I began to grieve for him. It was as if my father died for the second time.

In some of my loneliest moments, I wrote poems. Poems about love, poems about broken relationships, poems about loneliness, and poems about happiness were constant expressions of my feelings. The things I couldn't express audibly, the pains I couldn't share with anyone were written down. Whenever I was hurting the most, the thoughts plaguing my mind were the same.

"My life would be so different if you had lived."
The foundation of hell was firmly laid.

The Foundation Laid: The Flip Side

Those still left alive will rot away in enemy lands because
of their sins and the sins of their ancestors. "But at last my
people will confess their sins and the sins of their
ancestors for betraying me and being hostile toward me.
Leviticus 26:39-40

On a warm summer day of August 14, 1952, the fourth child was born to James and Dollie Johnson. Later, their fifth child would be born, Michael. This was in the fifties. Times were hard, the neighborhood was hard and my life would be hard. I had no idea what the world held for Henry Johnson. It was a time when very little was known about fetal alcohol syndrome or the dangers of drinking during pregnancy. At least, in our household, the dangers were unknown. No one thought twice about leaving open containers of alcoholic beverages around the house. This provided easy access for curious toddlers. I must have been four or five years old when I had my first taste of this life altering drug. The foundation for hell was forming.

As one of the youngest children, I would learn many lessons from my brother and sisters. My oldest brother taught me how to fight. My brother tried to fill in for my father who was rarely present in the home. He had more worldly interests. He served time with two great institutions, the military and the penal system. My mother struggled to take care of her five children. She was making minimum wage and improvising in the absence of the real head of the household. My needs were just one of many and not always a priority. At a young age, I learned how to acquire the things I needed. I don't remember how old I was when I first started stealing. The other children were wearing nice shoes and clothing. I had a desire for nice things, too. There was an older guy in the neighborhood I hung out with. He was stealing everything. There was a warehouse in the neighborhood. He liked to hit it. Stealing seemed to be the answer.

During my earliest years, we lived in the East Wynnton area of Columbus, Georgia. I attended Radcliff Elementary, the "school of hard knocks". This was a place to be knocked down. If you didn't know how to defend yourself, you got your lunch and milk money taken. I didn't plan to lose anything. Sometimes, the money would be used to buy ice cream from the lady next to the church, Ms. Gordy. As I grew older, I wondered if she was related to the infamous, Barry Gordy. She was a very organized businesswoman and the place was always spotless. All of the kids loved the woman with the good cream filled cookies and pink ice cream.

People from various backgrounds lived in the neighborhood. There were a variety of businesses lining the nearby blocks: Bob's Grocery, Eggin's Grocery, Jones' Café, the American Legion Post, and my favorite, the Flamingo Bar BQ. People inside and outside of the neighborhood loved this southern treat. The Flamingo was located on the corner of Radcliff Avenue and Buena Vista Road. In those days, you could get a small order of ribs for the grand total of fifty-two cents. The order came with two slices of bread cut diagonally and barbecue coleslaw. The cabbage was finely grated and seasoned with the famous sauce covering the ribs. At this time, it was considered the best barbecue in Columbus. The clientele verified this fact. There were always people outside waiting for her to open her doors. People came from across town for her ribs. Sometimes at the end of the evening, she had to turn customers away. The Flamingo is gone now.

Over the years, we saw celebrities visit the American Legion: B. B. King, Bobby Blue Bland, and Etta James, etc. Around the first of each month, the club would be packed to capacity. There were players, pimps, and prostitutes working to perfect their games. The robbers and burglars were also hard at work. Everybody was looking to fatten their pockets. The people frequenting the club had to park their cars several streets away. This made them easy prey for the criminals waiting for an easy target.

During the summers, I had a chance to follow the older kids. This gave me an opportunity to observe all the madness. We were allowed to stay out until 11 or 12:00 at night. However, we had to remain on our street, Spenola Street. The American Legion was in this range. It was right up the street from our house. This was appealing to young children looking for excitement. I was looking for excitement.

The club had an old beer cooler on the outside that was being disposed of. We used it as a platform. It elevated us to a height that allowed us to peer through the window of the club easily. From our position, we could observe everything happening inside. Sometimes, we watched our relatives as they socialized inside the club. If we became overly engrossed in what was happening on the other side of the window, we forgot about the club's security. Occasionally, the security guard would patrol the grounds, making sure the vehicles were secure. If he discovered us, he ran us away. As soon as he completed his rounds, we returned to our box office seat.

There is one memory still stands out in my mind. A lady lived down the street from our house. She loved to drink alcohol. I guess you can say she was an alcoholic. Sometimes, she drank more than her share. One night, we were looking into the window of the club. B. B. King was onstage performing with his band. Mrs. Edwards and her husband startled us. He was trying to persuade her to come home. She had other plans and she was determined to carry them out. She was going to leave her husband and follow B. B. King. The show was almost over. Mrs. Edwards had jumped on the bus with his driver and the security guards.

Mr. Edwards pleaded, "Please come home and leave these people alone."

He continued his attempts to pull her from the bus. Finally, they (Mr. Edwards, the bus driver, and security guards) were able to get the situation under control. The couple went home. She was still making her request known. She wanted to travel with B. B. King. After the show ended, B. B. King went on his way without a new addition to his tour.

A few years later, we moved to the south side of town, Kendrick Quarters. This was another rough neighborhood. In the early sixties, it seemed the police were afraid to come there. There was one gang called the Head Rag Gang. If you didn't have a problem (conflict or beef) with this gang, you were allowed to play baseball on the neighborhood playground. During this time, I developed my skills at the game. I was about ten or eleven. There were always games on the weekends. People from across Alabama and Georgia came to this neighborhood to play. These events were packed to capacity and there was only standing room. Jackie Robinson paved the way for Blacks to enter the major leagues, during this period. This increased the interest of people in the neighborhood for the sport. The teams competed using the best of their skills. They were very competitive. The prize appeared to be priceless. Their pride and reputations were at stake.

I played Little League baseball. My baseball coach really understood the game. My batting average increased and my ability to catch the ball improved. I lost my fear of catching a fast pitch or a hot shot grounder. However, it was around this same time I developed another skill. It wasn't in my family's budget to give me the things I wanted. I wasn't interested in working for the things I needed or wanted. By this time, I was accustomed to crime, drunkenness, and riotous living. These things were an intricate part of our neighborhood and my environment. There was always the option of choosing to be different. If I had searched diligently, perhaps, I would have found a positive role model. However, that's not the choice I made. I didn't have the role model.

There were small stores in the neighborhood that had homes adjacent to the stores. The store attendants would occasionally leave the stores unattended. Out of necessity, they would run home briefly to perform some task. Some of them had bells on the doors to alert them if someone entered the store. This was a simple problem to overcome. If I held the bell, they would never hear me creeping into the store. They often had cigar boxes or tackle boxes served as cash registers. The stores that had cash registers were careless, too. They would leave excessive amounts of cash available. Usually, cash was left lying on top of the register. Stealing enabled me to buy baseball gloves, footballs, and tennis shoes. Sometimes, I would attempt to bring the items home. My mother would question me about their origin. At first, I wasn't comfortable lying to her. It became easier to hide them or to let one of my friends keep the items. This scheming only led me to bigger endeavors.

There was another venture that proved profitable for me. At least, it seemed that way. We were renting our home from a man who lived in the house next door. Occasionally, when it was time to pay the rent, my mother would allow me to give him the money for her. I would follow her instruction carefully and return with her receipt. I was also watching him carefully. I observed where the landlord put the money before I left house. Was there any need for him to be concerned about a kid stealing from him? All of this worked in my favor. Who would expect a kid to ease through the bathroom window? He didn't. He kept the window open regularly.

When the opportunity presented, I waited until the landlord drove out the driveway. Then it was time to make my move. At first, I was a little hesitant. Fear tugged at me. They might return quickly. What if they had forgotten something? Casting aside the fear, I proceeded with my plan. I climbed through the open window and landed on the bathroom floor, being ever so careful to be quiet. My conscience was really working on me. There were so many 'what ifs.' I was almost ready to retreat back through the window. In the end, my greed won. I chose to ignore my fears. I carefully crept through the house until I found my target. I had last seen the money on the mantle piece. Bingo! There it was. I placed the money firmly in my pocket and trembled on to the door. At this point, I had another problem. There were houses on every side. Had anyone seen me enter the house? Had my plan been discovered? Were they waiting for me to exit the house?

Would I be identified as the culprit? I carefully peeped out the door. I didn't see anybody. At last, I made it back to the safety of my mother's home. The bathroom was the safest place for me to check my sting. What I had taken was exactly what I had given him, approximately $95. I couldn't give the money back to my mother. She wouldn't understand what I had done. I hid seventy-five dollars of the money in the house. With two ten-dollar bills hid in my socks, I headed outside.

Foolishness is bound in the heart of a child; but the rod of correction shall drive it far from him. Proverbs 22:15

Once outside, I found my friend Larry. We began splurging. We bought candy, sodas, hotdogs, and a football. Afterwards, Larry's grandmother called him into the house. Patiently, I waited on the porch for his return. I heard him screaming.

"Grandma, I don't know where he got the money from."

She was laying the strap to him. He had to run to get away from her. He ran out of the house. Larry lived across the street from my house. My mother must have known something. She was standing on the front porch and calling for me to come home. Reluctantly, I went, not knowing what to expect. Had I been implicated in the theft? She spoke plainly.

She asked me directly, "Henry did you get my money?"

What a relief; I still had a chance. I hadn't taken my mother's money. She had given me the money for the landlord. He had given me a receipt for her. What was my mother referring to? I was prolonging the inevitable. I took the whipping with ease, knowing it wouldn't last long. Afterwards, I sulked because I had been whipped for no reason. They had no proof. How was I implicated? I don't know. They never told me.

My sister Ann and sister-in-law Rosa accepted Jesus Christ as their Lord and Savior. They began attending a Pentecostal church. They went to the services every day. The joy in them began spreading through the family. My curiosity was peaked. I found myself going to church with them.

People were tarrying around the altar for the Holy Ghost. This was new to me and scary. People were on their knees calling on the name of Jesus. There were people standing behind them encouraging them to keep calling Jesus. There was a lot of shouting for joy. I didn't understand what I was feeling. My knees were hurting from bending them so long. I was glad to get up from the altar. In my haste to get up, I failed to receive the deliverance I needed desperately.

From my seat, I continued to observe as others received their deliverance. They were crying out for deliverance from all of their sins. Afterwards, they gathered into groups to talk about how they had been delivered. A lady came over to me and I almost ran out of the church. However, my sister showed up before I ran. This relieved some of my fear. The lady turned her attention back towards me.

My sister responded, "This is my brother Henry. The Lord has really blessed him."

The Lord really had blessed me. He had cured me from epilepsy. When I was younger, I would lapse into a daze and lose control of my bodily functions. When I came out of the trance, I was humiliated by what had happened. After observing one of my accidents, any girl who liked me looked at me in a different way. They looked at me with disgust. My mother took me to a specialist on several occasions. It seemed they didn't know what to prescribe for me. Each doctor referred me to another one. They kept performing tests looking for an answer. The tests never revealed the source of the seizures. On one occasion while in the doctor's office, I went into a trance. He was able to observe the occurrence first hand. Finally, he was able to prescribe the correct medication for the symptoms. After taking the medicine for a year, the seizures stopped.

After my fifth grade year, we moved to Beallwood Heights. My skills at playing baseball helped me adapt to the new neighborhood. I attended a church that had a baseball team. We played other teams in the city. The church provided us with transportation. I took my bad habits to the new neighborhood.

> *But understand this: If the owner of the house had known at what time of night the thief was coming, he would have kept watch and would not have let his house be broken into.* Matthew 24:43 (NIV)

People in this neighborhood were careless with their finances. I took advantages of their carelessness. One store was a convenient and regular target for me. Miss Julia's store was connected to her home. Whenever I caught her away from the store, I took advantage of the opportunity. I would use a Popsicle stick to pry the latch. She kept her money in a cigar box. I didn't take all of the money. Taking a little from her each time ensured I would be able to return another day. It was hard to keep track of the exact amount of money in the store using the cigar accounting system. If I had taken all the money, my tricks would have been easily discovered. Taking ten or twelve dollars each time was enough. This was a lot of money for me at the time.

When I was eleven years old, my tricks caught up with me. During this time, we were allowed to leave school for lunch. This was to allow you time to go home to eat. This was an acceptable practice for children who didn't have lunch money. The only requirement was you return before the lunch period ended. I walked into a trap during one of these times.

I left school with one of my friends. He had been breaking into teachers' houses. On this day, I went with him on his mission. I didn't know they were already watching him. We left school and went straight to a teacher's house. He broke the window and he eased into the house. From the inside of the house, he opened the door for me. We took watches, a small amount of money, and some food. We started back to school as if nothing had happened. When we arrived, we were about ten minutes late.

The accomplice of a thief is his own enemy;
he is put under oath and dare not testify.
Fear of man will prove to be a snare, but
whoever trusts in the LORD is kept safe.
Proverbs 29:24-25 NIV

The next day the administrators called us to the office. They questioned us about the burglary. We had a couple of the watches with us. They asked about them. We tried to lie, but to no avail. It just didn't add up. My fear confused me. I didn't know how serious it was. Most of my thoughts centered on my mother and father. What would they do when they found out? A number of things were going through my mind. Did he tell somebody? Did someone recognize the watches?

There was a detective called to the office. We were taken into custody. The detective took us out of the school. There were children in the hall looking at us as we walked down the hall. Once outside, we were placed in the backseat of the car. My thoughts became more crowded. What was going to happen to us? I didn't feel in charge. They had the upper hand. My games had caught up with me. This time it wasn't my plan. I had only followed my friend and was caught up in the moment. I tried to act tough and cool. They didn't need to know I was scared. The older guys had trained me well.

"Never tell (snitch) on anyone else. Don't act scared if you are caught. Don't let the police or jail scare you. They'll try to get you to tell on other people. Don't let them trick you. They can't be trusted. Don't let anybody trick you in the jail. If anybody tries to take advantage of you be ready to fight."

I remembered everything they had said. However, I had other thoughts. How long would I be away from my family? We were questioned again. This was when I learned my friend had committed other burglaries. They tried to scare us. The detectives already knew my friend. He had been to juvenile camp before. They contacted our parents about the charges. After all the paperwork was processed, our parents had to pick us up from the police station. We were scheduled to appear in juvenile court at a future date.

When I got home, I got two whippings. My mother got me first. I was licking my wounds and feeling sorry for myself. My father wasn't home yet. It wasn't over. She showed me a little mercy. However, when Daddy got me, he laid it on. The beating helped me. It taught me to be more cautious in the future.

The judge sentenced me to a week at the Juvenile Detention Center. It was my friend's second trip. This merited him two weeks. This was a new experience for me. At night, you could hear the kids crying. In the daytime, everybody faked being strong and tough. Under the cloud of night, you couldn't tell who was crying. I refused to cry. Not one tear ever fell from my eyes. What I learned from the older guys kept me determined to stay my course. I would show no sign of weakness. The things they taught me would return to taunt me. For almost a year, I went straight.

In those days, Afros were the main hairstyle, or in my case, the nappy head. My hair was long and coarse. I didn't want my mother to do anything with it. In my efforts to keep her away from my hair, I would comb the top of my hair. However, underneath my hair was untouched. This is what contributed to my nickname 'Buckwheat.' This was during my sixth grade year. I didn't like the name, but it stuck. Whenever someone called me this name, they risked a sharp reply.

The foundation of hell was firmly in place.

Building Walls

If she be a wall, we will build upon her a palace of silver: and if she be a door, we will enclose her with boards of cedar. Song of Solomon 8:9

On October 2, 1974, at age 15, my first pregnancy resulted in the birth of an 8 pounds 5 ounces baby girl, Earline. I emphasize first because the neighborhood gossip mill had accused me of being pregnant several times. My baby was born within an hour of my arrival at the hospital. A few weeks after my baby's birth, I began attending Columbus High School. I started the 9th grade over. This would be a new beginning in several ways. My Saturday shopping trips were limited. My mother had another person to provide for, my child. I resented my weekly shopping trips ending. I would still be able to go shopping, but not as frequently.

In the meantime, I became increasingly convinced I wanted to be treated like an adult. Trying to ease the pain and lonesomeness, I began mild experimentation with beer and marijuana, but I really didn't like either one of them. I was still trying to find a place to fit to no avail. The gap between my mother and me was growing wider. Mama didn't know anything about drugs, but it was obvious to her something was wrong with me. She tried to figure it out. However, when she tried, she was wrong every time.

"You have been smoking marijuana."

This was on the day when I had been drinking. On the days when I had smoked marijuana, she got it wrong again.

"You're drunk! You've been drinking."

One night when I was attempting to leave the house, Mama threatened to call the police if I left. This threat didn't go over well with me. She was bluffing and I called her bluff. After she refused to call the police, I called them for her. When the police arrived, Mama was crying and I spoke to the policeman.

"This is my mother. She wanted to call you because I won't stay at home."

After making this statement, I walked off. I went to Ma'Dear's house. Ma'Dear would never turn me away. It didn't matter what happened. I told her Mama had put me out again. In my mind, she had kicked me out. She wouldn't let me stay there on my own terms.

Mama often said, "Two grown people can't live under one roof. Somebody has to be the child."

She didn't mean this literally and never planned for me to move out, but this made perfect sense to me. There was no way I was going to act like a child. After all, I had a child. I moved in with Ma'Dear temporarily, for less than a couple of weeks. Almost immediately, I secured a job at a local cotton mill, working second shift. Two of my cousins were already working there.

Within a month, at sixteen, I got my first apartment and moved out on my own. My great grandmother was able to help me in securing the apartment. She knew the landlord. The rent was $65 a month. I moved into a two-bedroom apartment downtown. My apartment, number twelve, was upstairs. The apartment building was located behind a nightclub. Adjacent to the club was a liquor store.

There was a neighborhood grocery store across the street. Additionally, there were several clubs in the area.

By lying about my age, I was able to secure credit at several furniture stores to furnish the apartment. My bedroom was decorated in black and red. The walls were painted black. The center of attention in the room was my queen size waterbed covered with a red spread. The waterbed was one of my first purchases. This was something I had wanted since seventh grade. Mama refused to purchase the bed for my birthday. She opted for an Early American bedroom suit. It was nice, but it wasn't a waterbed. At last, I had one.

Next door to me, there lived three elderly gentlemen. They each had a charge account with the liquor store and the grocery store. They also had a fascination for their new neighbor. They drank alcohol every day. They also wanted me to drink with them. This gave me an idea.

It would be nice to have a huge party. With a little help from these gentlemen, I wouldn't have to buy anything. They were already using each of their accounts to impress me. Each day, they would come to my apartment with something. They tried to compete with each other.

They tried to feed me alcohol. It was funny. They never knew I wasn't drinking any of it. I hated the smell of gin. I insisted I drank my liquor straight, with no chaser. In my bedroom, I kept their empty bottles. Inside my closet was a big box. The box was used to collect bottles of alcohol. In my bedroom, I also kept paper cups. These served as funnels. When they poured my cup of liquor, I pretended to drink it. Inevitably, I went to the bedroom where I poured the liquor into one of the bottles in the bedroom. Afterwards, I returned to the living room for another cup. It didn't take long before they had bought enough food and alcohol for the party.

In junior high school, one of my friends began selling drugs. He bought a new car. This impressed everybody. At this time, he had been selling drugs for several years. He bought me a charcoal lace dress. The dress was long, but it clung to me in all the right places. It was perfect for the party.

The night of the party, people arrived quickly. The house was packed. That's all I remember about the party. The next morning, I woke up laying across the waterbed in my expensive dress. This was the night I decided to drink some of the gin. The punch was loaded with it. It didn't take much for me to pass out. I continued to take the liquor from the old men, but I didn't drink it.

Several months later, the waterbed burst. The water flooded my apartment and the one below it. My love for waterbeds was cured.

It became harder to maintain my job and continue in school. During my breaks at the mill, I tried to complete my homework. It was after midnight before I dropped off to sleep each night. Most of my time at school was spent sleeping. Earline stayed with Ma'Dear during the week to make it easier on me.

My troubles at work increased, as two men made unwanted and unwarranted advances towards me. The first advance resulted in my having to walk several miles home to avoid being raped. At 11:30 p.m., I jumped out of the car and started walking home. My anger made the walk easier. I was too angry to focus on how tired I was. The time was well after midnight when I made it safely home. I never spoke to him again.

On a Sunday afternoon, the second man showed up on the doorstep of my apartment, demanding I open the door for him. From the window of my apartment, I watched as he continued his threats. How had he learned my address? He eventually left, after I refused to open the door. The next day at work, there was a confrontation and a fight with his wife. In the end, we were both terminated. It wasn't long before she was rehired. I tried to get my job back, but was unsuccessful.

Job or no job, my mind was made up; I wasn't going back home. This was about the time I met a man fifteen years older than I was. He was good looking and this was what basically attracted me to him. We began to date. Shortly thereafter, he moved in with me. I had opened the door to hell. The relationship very quickly became extremely abusive. He began abusing me physically and emotionally. He was obsessively jealous and in my confused mind, I thought this was love. I had no idea what love was or what I had gotten myself into.

Robert Hall was a small man, about 5'5" and less than 130 lbs. He was a man with an obvious Napoleon Complex. This 'Small Man Complex' causes a man who is small in statue to struggle to prove his manhood, usually by exerting power or authority over a person he deems weaker or inferior.

My great grandmother, Mae was able to get me a job working at an appliance store. This job ended abruptly, too. After being on the job for two days, there was another confrontation. I was hired to clean the store. This seemed easy enough. Part of my duties included keeping the showroom clean. Several times a day, I went over the floor with a damp mop. One of the men called me to the showroom. The store was open and customers were coming in and out of the store. He pointed to a couple of small scuffmarks on the floor. With the mop, I attempted to get the marks up, but they wouldn't budge.

"Maybe you should put some elbow grease to it."

Bearing down as hard as I could on the mop, I went over the spots again. Still, they didn't move.

"No! I mean you should really put some elbow grease to it. You need to get closer to the spots."

After it became clear to me what he meant, I responded very sweetly.

"Sir, can you please show me what you mean?"

"We won't be needing your services anymore."

He wanted me to scrub the floor on my knees. I didn't need the job that bad. My great grandmother begged me to apologize. She had worked for their family for years. I had done nothing wrong and I wasn't going to beg.

At seventeen, I began working at the Mayfair Lounge. I wasn't old enough to sell alcoholic beverages, but Robert worked this out with the manager. This lounge led me through the corridors of hell. I still hadn't developed a taste for alcohol, but I kept trying to get the hang of it. After all, I was involved with an alcoholic.

Shortly after my eighteenth birthday, I married Robert Hall. This was my second major mistake. The first was becoming involved with him. Not only was he an alcoholic and abusive, he was extremely promiscuous. My mother begged me not to marry him. As usual, I wasn't going to listen to Mama.

In January 1978, I earned my GED and began attending technical college. Still without a clue to what I wanted to do with my life, I enrolled in the Electronics Technology Program. In spite of the problems in my relationship with Robert, I managed to complete one quarter of the program. By the next quarter, my life would move in a different direction and to a different city.

The relationship with Robert could only be characterized as a series of hurricanes. The beatings were often public, to include several at the Mayfair. The police were called on a continuous basis throughout the relationship. There were several attempts to kill him in response to the beatings. After a confrontation with him, I left almost everything I owned and moved to Atlanta, Georgia. My journey was taking me down another corridor in hell.

While working at the Mayfair, I met a pimp who was also a drug dealer, Jim (not his real name), who lived in Atlanta. However, he was from Columbus. He drove a new money–green colored Seville. He was my biggest tipper, whenever he was in town. Whenever he was in the club, I could expect at least $40 from him. Often, he would buy drinks for everyone in the nightclub. It didn't matter if he knew them. Liking his generosity, or his ability to flaunt his money, I would tease him.

"If I ever decide to work the streets, I am going to find you."

This wasn't my intention in leaving Columbus, but upon my arrival in Atlanta, I was broke and my car needed minor repairs. There was one person in the city I knew who would be willing to get the car repaired. This would also provide an opportunity to have some fun. It was thus that my ignorance took me down to Peachtree Street looking for Jim. This was actually my second time visiting him in Atlanta. The first visit left me determined to learn to drive. He had asked me to drive his car. I had never driven a car before. When I left Atlanta, I was determined to drive his car the next time I saw him.

Jim wasn't tall, pretty, handsome, good looking or fine. Looking at him didn't make me weak at the knees. He didn't woo me with a smooth line and it wasn't that he had perfected the mac-game (pimp-game). Actually, he didn't fit any of the stereotypes commonly portrayed in the media. My curiosity coupled with desperation caused me to seek refuge in the wrong place, the streets. The chaos in my life kept me in the relationship.

Jim was very special in his own right. Anyone expecting a relationship with him would have to understand there was a lot of baggage coming with the relationship. The baggage came in the form of women and drugs. He never said this verbally, but the signs were obvious. He had every intention of being with a different woman every night. These didn't mean anything to him. These aren't the relationships I am referencing. They were only strokes to his ego and an effort to satisfy the perversion of his flesh.

The women who came with the package were the ones who had been considered his women. He believed he branded each of them for life. Hindsight tells me it was the other way around. Each woman marked him forever. He kept the door open for each of them to return. He loved the telephone and seemed to think it was invented just for him. He made regular telephone calls to the women who passed through his life. I was getting ready to make my own mark on his life. He liked being in control and so did I. Early in our relationship, I learned this key to survival: let him think he's in charge.

In those days there was no king in Israel:
every man did what was right in his own
eyes. Judges 21:25

While living in Atlanta, I left Earline with Aunt Bobbie. This kept her away from my wayward lifestyle. My aunt and Earline became the best of friends. To put it nicely, they were both great debaters. They argued all the time. Yet, they were inseparable. My aunt often referred to

Earline as F. Lee Bailey. From the age of two years old, Earline wanted to be lawyer. She worked on her oral arguments with my aunt. During one phase of their relationship, my aunt developed a favorite saying. She repeated this answer to everything said to her.

"It don't matter."

This was a source of irritation for Earline. She hated this worse than being called F. Lee Bailey. One day Aunt Bobbie asked Earline a question.

"What's wrong with you, Earline?"

"It don't matter! It don't matter! It don't matter! That's all you know, 'It don't matter.'"

I had another name for their relationship. They were beer-buddies. Without fail, my aunt stopped by the store each day, as she returned home from work. She purchased at least one six pack of beer. As soon as she started drinking, Sonya (her daughter) and I made our nightly getaway. Earline shared at least one of the beers with my aunt. Once, my aunt walked into the kitchen in the middle of the night. Earline was in the kitchen. Sitting on the kitchen table was a beer can. When Earline saw her, she had a request.

"Big Bobbie, tell me where the mop is."

"What do you need with the mop?"

"Just tell me where the mop is."

From the refrigerator to the table, there was a trail of red liquid. Earline had poured Kool-Aid into the beer can.

We traveled from Atlanta to Columbus at least once a month. Aunt Bobbie always rode with us. Before leaving to return to Atlanta, she was sure to spend time with her niece, Mama. This was always interesting to watch. They were more like sisters. During the early years of their lives, they had been raised in the same house or next door to each other. Aunt Bobbie often teased Mama about her obsession with neatness. Mama didn't seem to get the joke. Aunt Bobbie told this story.

"When Herman (my father) died, Jimmy Lee came by the house to see Evelyn. She had three pillows stacked neatly in the corner of the sofa. He said, 'I'm sorry about Herman.' He was getting ready to sit on the pillows as he said this. Evelyn responded, 'That's okay, just don't sit on those pillows.'"

The pillows on the sofa were so perfect someone remarked, "I thought you pinned them together."

This was another one of her favorite stories, "Once when I came to Columbus, I stayed with Evelyn. She left me at the house when she went to work. I was tired and sleepy. I looked at the sofa and the pillows were stacked neatly in each corner. I said, 'No I can't sleep there.' I went into the bedroom and everything was in place. I knew I couldn't fix everything the way she had left it. Finally, I went into the bathroom. I looked around and decided the best place for my nap was in the bath tub."

Aunt Bobbie told everybody this story. One time she came to visit from Atlanta and brought a friend with her. They were sitting on Ma'Dear's porch drinking a case of beer. Mama was at home, on the other side of Warren Williams. The ditch divides the project into two sections. As they were drinking, Aunt Bobbie was telling the stories about Mama. The fact that her friend believed her caused the stories to become more fantastic.

"Now, we couldn't do this at Evelyn's house. If she was here, she would be constantly cleaning up. When Pickle (my mother's sister) was dating, she would be sitting on one end of the sofa with her boyfriend while Evelyn was straightening up the other end. At her house, you'll see pretty ashtrays sitting around, but those aren't the ones you use. She has some more in the pantry. They are pretty too, but she'll let you put ashes in them. The only thing is she's going to stand next to you as you smoke. Every time you dump the cigarette, she's going to take the ashtray, wash it, dry it out, and give it back to you. When you go to her house, even if it's raining, she not going to let you in; until, she sprays every room in the house, with air freshener. If you ask to use the bathroom, she's going to give you a can of air freshener. Everything is spotless and she has white carpet. When you go in the house you have to take your shoes off and leave them by the door."

They sat there with my aunt spinning these tales until they drank the case of beer. My aunt never got drunk until she saw the last can of beer. It started to rain. My aunt was feeling pretty good and wanted to prove her point. She took the lady to Mama's house. I drove them to the other side of the project, across the ditch. By this time, it was raining a little harder. My aunt knocked on the door.

"Listen! You hear her spraying?"

True to form, Mama was spraying air freshener. Mama never let anybody in the house without spraying every room in the house. It didn't matter if it was raining. This included her children. We had keys to the house. However, whenever she was home the screen door was locked. It didn't matter if we were in the yard. On more than one occasion, I had stood outside in the rain begging her to open the door.

"Mama! Please stop spraying and open the door. It's me. It's raining."

The lady was convinced Aunt Bobbie was telling the truth. When they walked in the house, the lady took off her shoes. Mama was standing there confused, as Aunt Bobbie burst into laughter.

"You don't have to take your shoes off. Bobbie what did you tell her? Don't believe this girl."

Mama couldn't convince the lady. She had to use the bathroom, but she was afraid to ask. Aunt Bobbie had exaggerated. However, part of what she said was true. Mama wasn't "saved" then. There were ashtrays in various parts of the house. These were just for decoration. There were other ashtrays stacked neatly in the pantry. Whenever someone wanted to smoke in the house, Mama would get one from the pantry. They weren't cheap ashtrays, but they were ones she didn't like as well. She would wash an ashtray ten times before you finished the first cigarette. I thought it was enough to make anybody quit smoking. Pickle said Mama regularly cleaned up as she sat in the living room with her dates. I don't remember any of this. However, I remember Aunt Pickle dancing in the living room all night long with her friends. She could twist all the way down to the floor and back up.

Mama also had another habit. Each time she cooked she preformed this ritual. Whenever we left the house, she went through this routine. Sometimes, she would return to the house and go through the routine again. She stopped at the stove. She went from one knob to the other.

"Off, off, off, off, off, off, off, off, off, off..."

Each time, she said 'off' ten times. We had a double oven. When she finished with the stove, she went to the door. She shook the knob so hard, we thought it would break.

There was always a cooler of beer traveling with us on our trips to Columbus. Aunt Bobbie didn't believe in travelling without it. Earline and my aunt rode in the back seat of the car. They drank beer and argued during the entire trip. On one of these trips, Earline decided she would drink more than the allotted one can of beer. As I was driving down the expressway, I heard the second can of beer pop.

"Earline don't touch another can of beer!"

"I'm never going to stop drinking beer. When we get to Columbus, I'm going to get me a beer and some hot peanuts."

This was the normal routine upon our arrival. However, in the near future, Earline was going to change her declaration.

After being with Jim for about six months, I reconciled with Robert and he moved to Atlanta. It wasn't long before Jim moved back to Columbus. Robert began abusing me again and I followed Jim to Columbus. We had been in Columbus for a few months when Jim decided to take a trip to New York. I decided to follow him. This was around June of 1979. After a few months of riotous living in New York City, it was necessary for us to make a hasty retreat back to Columbus. While we were in New York, Jim developed a new habit: free basing cocaine. This hastened circumstances sending me off to renew my relationship with Robert. This dreadful mistake almost cost my life. It was a deadly cycle.

> *The LORD is my rock, and my fortress, and my deliverer; my God, my strength, in whom I will trust; my buckler, and the horn of my salvation, and my high tower. I will call upon the LORD, who is worthy to be praised: so shall I be saved from mine enemies. The sorrows of death compassed me, and the floods of ungodly men made me afraid. The sorrows of hell compassed me about: the snares of death prevented me. In my distress I called upon the LORD, and cried unto my*

*God: he heard my voice out of his temple,
and my cry came before him, even into his
ears.* Psalm 18:2-6

In February 1980, a life spinning towards hell for years found its destination. Shortly after reconciling with Robert, the relationship became abusive again. We were living in Atlanta at the time. One of the beatings resulted in my life being changed forever. Physical scars would also mark my body forever. The beating ended when my body was severely burned. It was also the first time I heard God speak audibly.

My gown was burning. However, it seemed like the whole room was full of flames and I was in the middle of an unquenchable fire. This was a glimpse of hell. I jumped up and began to pull the negligee over my head. When the remnants of the gown were nearing my eyes, an authoritative voice spoke from heaven.

"Pull it back down."

I obeyed without a second thought.

*But I cried to Him, My God, who lives forever,
don't take my life while I am still so young!*
Psalm 102:24 (NLT)

When I woke up in the Intensive Care Unit of the Burn Unit at Grady Hospital, I was drowsy and in severe pain. I was told second and third degree burns covered 70% of my body, but I had no idea what a second or third degree burn was. My wildest imagination couldn't envision what this meant. I understood I was still alive and this was about the depth of my understanding. I had no idea how serious my condition was or that my life was still in jeopardy.

My first stay at Grady lasted three months and five days. It's not that I remember this, since I was heavily medicated most of the time I was in the hospital. The medication affected portions of my memory, or perhaps I deliberately chose to block out some of the pain. My mother has filled in the gaps for most of what happened that year. Actually, it seems I lost a year of my life, the year so many look forward to, the twenty-first year. Several months after my release from the hospital, I was able to read my hospital records.

And suddenly there shined round about him
a light from heaven. Acts 9:3

One night, someone patting my hand awakened me from my sleep. Upon opening my eyes, I was surprised, but not afraid to see only a brilliant light. There was an incredible sense of peace in my room. This light enabled me to see my body for the first time in its entirety. Until this time, most of my movements had been confined to being flipped on my circular bed or being transferred from my bed to a stretcher. Whenever I would leave the room, I was headed to the patient elevator. Having lived in Columbus most of my life, I wasn't familiar with the hospital.

The hand of the Lord was upon me, and
carried me out in the spirit of the Lord, and
set me down in the midst of the valley which
was full of bones, and caused me to pass by
them round about: and, behold, there were
very many in the open valley; and, lo, they
were very dry. And he said unto me, Son of
man, can these bones live? And I answered,
O Lord God, Thou knoweth. Again he said
unto me, Prophesy upon these bones, and
say unto them, O ye dry bones, hear the
word of the Lord. Thus saith the Lord God
unto these bones; Behold, I will cause breath
to enter into you, and ye shall live: And I will

lay sinews upon you and bring flesh upon
you, and cover you with skin, and put breath
in you, and ye shall live; and ye shall know
that I am the Lord. Ezekiel 37:1-6

This night, I saw a different part of the hospital. We left the room heading to a different elevator, the public elevator. This magnificent calming light took me from the room to the passenger elevator. We boarded this elevator and went down to the main entrance of Grady. The light guided me down a flight of stairs and out the front of the hospital. We took a journey from Atlanta to Columbus via the expressway. On the way to Columbus, I saw my life before my entering the hospital. All of my sins were candidly revealed to me. There were scenes from Peachtree, scenes from Columbus, and scenes from New York City. Clearly manifested to me was the wickedness of my lifestyle. There was no doubt this lifestyle led directly to hell.

Once we arrived in Columbus at Warren Williams Apartments the nature of the scenes changed. Along with my mother and my daughter, I was heading to church. I was walking to the car with them. The light took me back up the expressway and along the way. I saw what my life would be like in the future. I was going to live. I was going to recover. We returned to Grady, entering through a back door of the hospital. We went down the hall to the elevator. Once inside the elevator, a finger reached over and pushed the button for the tenth floor. The light returned me to the room and gently placed me back in the bed. Through all of this, I wasn't afraid. There was no need to be afraid.

For I neither received it of man, neither was I
taught it, but by the revelation of Jesus
Christ. Galatians 1:12

It was obvious Jesus wanted to save me. Me! In all of my filthiness, all of my wretchedness, He wanted to save me. Me! He had died for me. He died for damaged goods. There was nothing lovable about me. I didn't even love me. There was nothing morally good about me. Yet for this Charlotte, He had died. It wasn't for a Charlotte who was nice and clean, but for one who was a Black Sheep. He had laid down His life willingly for me. Me! He died for me. In all of my misery, He died for me. He had forgiven me for everything I had ever done.

My condition prevented me from being able to live alone. The things that had troubled and depressed me before the fire were insignificant. Before, I had worried about not being able to take care of my daughter. Now, I couldn't take care of either of us. It was necessary for me to return to my mother's house, the place I left at sixteen. My return was totally different from the way I left. I left to be independent before reaching the age of maturity. At the age of maturity, I was returning, totally dependent.

For over a year, I had no income, no insurance, and no food stamps. My mother provided for all my needs and Ma'Dear pitched in. The doctors at Grady gave me the name of a doctor in Columbus to contact. When we contacted the doctor, he arranged for me to receive extended physical and occupational therapy without payment. The doctors at Grady had started the process for me to draw disability income. This was a hard battle. Legal Aid appointed me a lawyer to assist with the case. The battle was fought over a year. My claim was turned down repeatedly. When I went for my final hearing, God blessed me. Before the hearing began the judge walked into the hall and asked me to come into his office. My mother and attorney were with me. He shocked us all with his comments.

"You have suffered enough. There is no doubt you are disabled. This was clear from the moment the claim was filed. There are a number of questions I have to ask you. I'm going to go over those with you. Afterwards, I want you to return to the hall and I'll call you back in. I'll turn on the tape recorder to record the session. In the end, I'll approve the claim."

After we moved back to Columbus, my Aunt Bobbie would come down sometimes to visit. Earline and Aunt Bobbie were no longer "Beer Buddies". Earline had committed her life to God and she no longer drank beer. Whenever Bobbie came to town, she would stay up all night talking to Mama. One night while they were doing this, Earline woke up. I was asleep in the other bedroom, trying to ignore the all night ritual. Earline had a message from heaven for Aunt Bobbie. With the boldness of the Apostle Paul, she delivered the message.

"Aunt Bobbie you need to stop drinking beer and you need to stop messing with that deacon. He's a deacon in the church and he has no business messing with you. You need to give your life to Jesus. I don't mean just going to church. You need to live right."

Aunt Bobbie in her usual form responded, "But Earline, I need somebody to take care of me and somebody to hold me."

Earline responded with conviction, "You have a job. You can take care of yourself and God will hold you."

The answer from Aunt Bobbie came back, "Well Earline, I have one beer left up to Mae's (Bobbie's mother) house. After I drink that one, I'll stop drinking."

Before she went back off to sleep, Earline told her, "Pour it out or whatever you need to do, but don't drink it."

Earline was about five years old during this exchange. Aunt Bobbie drank other beers, but she said she didn't drink that one and she gave up the deacon. Years later, she quit drinking and smoking for good.

Aunt Bobbie was the one who stuck by me during some of the most difficult times in my life. She meddled in my life to the point of obsession. She was also my biggest supporter when I released my first book, *A Journey to Hell and Back*. She was seriously ill when the book was released. However, she ignored her own health to promote my book. During the final days of her life, she promoted my book from her bed in intensive care. It was only hours before her death when she finally relented, allowing me to remove the books she had displayed around her room.

In my zealous attempt to be the ideal Christian, I reconciled with Robert. Within a few months of the reconciliation, I realized I had again made a dreadful mistake. My questions concerning marriage relationships escalated. The answers to my questions came back the same each time.

"Marriage is a permanent covenant. Christians are supposed to win the unsaved spouse."

With the emotional and physical abuse continuing, it was hard for me to reconcile the God who had forgiven me for all my wretchedness, with the one who wouldn't forgive me choosing the wrong spouse. Slowly, I began to feel isolated within the church. Although, I continued to attend services faithfully, I was moving further from a God who was punishing me for marrying this horribly brutal man. With everything within me, I was trying to live up to what I thought God expected of me. Without a doubt, I was failing to achieve these false expectations. It was apparent either he was going to kill me or I was going to kill him. Once I made up my mind to put him out permanently, I felt like a complete failure as a Christian.

Your words have been stout against me, saith the Lord. Yet ye say, What have we spoken so much against thee? Ye have said, It is in vain to serve God: and what profit is it that we have kept His ordinance, and that we have walked mournfully before the Lord of host? Malachi 3:13-14

To make matters even more complicated God was about to perform a miracle in my body. My daughter was the only child, only grandchild, and only great-grandchild. However, at the age of five, she had committed her life to God. At age seven, she had begun to pray for a miracle, she was lonely and tired of being the only child. She prayed her mother would become pregnant. To my astonishment, God granted her request and I conceived, after I had decided to end the marriage.

On January 3, 1983, after twenty-three hours of labor, I gave birth to a healthy baby boy, Herman Alexander Hall. He was named after my father and my grandmother. This was my miracle baby. However, this child couldn't save a marriage doomed from the beginning. Convinced I had failed as a Christian, I returned to the familiarity of the streets. Like a bad penny, within days, Jim moved back to Columbus.

In my heart, there was a wall against God.

Building Walls: The Flip Side

For all the riches which God hath taken from our father, that is ours, and our children's: now then, whatsoever God hath said unto thee, do. Genesis 31:16

When I was sixteen or seventeen, I picked up a new habit that would control my life, for years to come. This habit would keep me in a cycle of revolving in and out of the prison system. It's a cycle of drugs, crime, prison, release, drugs, crime, and so it continues. The cycle seems as if it has no beginning, and it threatens never to end. It's a cycle that threatens to destroy family, friends, relationships, society, dignity, and human worth. It's a cycle that will make you hate yourself. It will make you curse the day you were born. It's a cycle that will make you hate the day and beg for the night. It's a cycle that will keep your body at war with your mind. It's a cycle that breeds corruption and deceit. The cycle causes infidelity and greed. It's a cycle that leads you to submit when your mind says no, but your body is saying yes. It's a cycle that distorts reality and time. The cycle spins and spins until it controls your mind, your thoughts, and actions. It's a cycle that turns fathers against sons and daughters. It's a cycle that causes a mother to question her skills at motherhood. It's a cycle that causes blame and guilt. It's a cycle God alone can break.

Along with several friends, I had been stealing. I had been stealing for years. However, I hadn't been stealing with this group. When they sold the merchandise, they accepted payment in a way I hadn't expected. Instead of money, they accepted drugs. I didn't want to lose my portion of the profits. My greed led me to accept a portion of the drugs as my cut. This was the day I was introduced to heroin. It was the day the walls of the cycle were cemented together. The day threatened to destroy my life forever. This habit will be referred to as my monkey because it's always on my back.

In 1971, I was sent to a camp for youthful offenders. This didn't change anything about my behavior. I left this camp resolved to continue my life of crime. After my release, I really got into selling drugs. In approximately six months, I was locked up again.

This time I went to a real prison. At this camp, they worked me like a dog. We had to build fishponds. There was no machinery, only picks and shovels. We started planning our escape. However, they had officers who were expert marksmen. This camp was strict. I stayed at the camp two years.

Finally, I was transferred to a county camp. Being in a county camp is hard, but it's better than a state camp. In a county camp the rules are more relaxed. This made it easier to sneak drugs into the prison and have unauthorized conjugal visits. The inmates were allowed to receive meals prepared by their family during visitation time and carry cash money. Inmates were allowed to have up to $20 on hand in cash. This made it easier to conduct illegal money transactions. In prison, there were many entrepreneurs. People indulged in drug trafficking, loan sharking, gambling, marketing personal items from home, janitorial services, and other personal services such as ironing and hair cutting. The people who had money from home or business ventures within the prison had the opportunity to exploit those who were economically dependent. There were also paid work details available to bring in additional money.

The guards and staff are less formal with the inmates in this type of institution. Although there is still a power differential, the staff still recognizes the humanity of the inmates. In a state camp, the inmates are often treated as savages without any moral or redeeming value. This dehumanizing treatment can have lasting effects on the self-esteem of those forced to experience it.

Actually, we made the choice. We chose to commit the crimes that ultimately lead to incarceration. Nevertheless, after being in the system repeatedly, it becomes less of a choice. At least on the surface, it seems this way. After years of being treated like a savage, you start to respond like one. You lose all hope in any redeeming value in yourself. It appears the streets are the only place you can acquire a decent job. Prison is the only place you can gain respect. If you portray yourself as a professional with no weakness in your game, the other inmates will respect you. There is additional respect if you avoid the homosexual activity. On the streets, this respect is not readily available to an ex-convict.

There are physical drawbacks to being in any camp. They often lack modern conveniences, like central air-conditioning. Many of the newer prisons are made of metal fabrications. The temperatures inside the facilities are often exceptionally hot or cold. The food served consists of high quantities of starch and soybeans. In many of the counties the prison is the only major industry and the leading employer. Ultimately, this attracts some people who are ill prepared to work in any capacity with people. Some of them thrive on the authority or power over the inmates. Some officers insist on your standing at attention when they pass. You are instructed to call them

"Sir." Your failures to comply can result in disciplinary actions. Some officers operate on a fear factor. They are afraid of the inmate population. To mask their fear, they antagonize the inmates. If the inmate responds negatively, he has a group of officers at his disposal to beat the inmate down. The low paying positions often tempt the officers to engage in shady activities with inmates. This includes bringing drugs into the prison.

Additionally, there are emotional drawbacks. Your life is taken totally out your control. Strangers who have no interest in your emotional wellbeing are given control over your future. From the time you enter the system, you are just a number, not a person. You are told what to wear, how to wear it, where to sleep, when to sleep, when to wake up, when to bathe, when to watch television, who to share a room with, what to eat, where to eat, and how to eat. If there is unwanted food on your tray, you are told who not to share it with. In wishing for time to pass quickly, you wish your life away. Years are subtracted from your life, as you grow older behind the bars. On the outside of the prison, life goes on without you. Your family gets older. People get sick and people die. Circumstances often prevent you from attending the funerals. Inside the prison, you also watch people die. My brother Michael and I had one desire. We didn't want to die in prison. We had a lot of feelings about prison. However, our feelings were strongest about dying in prison.

It was a game, a game of intimidation and a game of fear. Each side was committed. Each side was determined. I will show no signs of intimidation. I will show no signs of fear. The inmates played it. The guards played it. Ultimately, each one walked into the prison not knowing how they would leave, not knowing when they would leave. They didn't know if the prison would be the place where they died in.

After I was in the county camp for almost three months, my father died. They allowed me to go home for three days on a pass for the funeral. My mother guaranteed my return to the prison. Out of respect for her, I returned as promised. However, freedom was on my mind. Rumors were traveling back to the prison about how well things in the drug trade were going in New York. A number of inmates from Columbus began making plans to escape. I was the first one to leave. With very little effort, I made it to New York.

After selling drugs for a period of time, I started stealing again. Eventually, the stealing caught up with me. I was busted three times in New York. The third time, they took my fingerprints. When they ran my prints, the charges from Georgia came up. For six months, I was locked up at Rikers Island. The sheriff's department from Georgia picked me up on the 179th day and returned me to the state. After returning to Georgia, I was sent across the state to another county camp. After about eighteen months, I was paroled. When I was released, the cycle repeated.

In 1979, I was in a county camp in Georgia. It was here that I met a young lady from Atlanta. I met her through a guy who was serving time at the same camp. Valerie was nice looking, a sharp dresser, and had a decent personality. She also had a good job. My friend provided me with this information before I met her. In prison, it very common for inmates to introduce each other to people on the outside. These people are often exploited for the inmates' needs. While in prison it is important to receive money, letters, visits, and gift packages from the outside. This provides the inmate with emotional support and serves as a status symbol. Valerie started coming to visit me at the prison. After getting aquatinted with her, I thought this might be someone with whom I could spend my life.

Previously, I had served time at this camp. I had also escaped from the camp before. Freedom started lingering on my mind. It seemed a good idea to put some of my time on an installment plan. I decided I was not going to complete my sentence at this time. I decided to release myself from the penal system and to return only if I was caught. My decision to leave was not influenced by relationship with Valerie.

My work detail involved working in the shop next to the prison. For about three months, I saved my money. I sent word for a friend to pick me up near the prison. The garbage trucks provided easy access for a ride away from the prison. After checking the route for each truck, I decided which one I would use for my escape. The hopper of the truck would make a perfect hiding place. The inmates working the back of the truck wouldn't give me away. I waited for a week for my friend to get back with me. After I didn't hear from him, I had to adjust my plan. I asked Valerie to pick me up at the shop. She drove down the side street and turned around. When she returned, I jumped in the back seat and laid down. It went off without a hitch.

After making sure we hadn't been followed, she took me to a friend's house. My friend was expecting me. She called another friend to come get me. He picked me up from her house and hid me until about nine that night. He drove me to Atlanta to a mall. Another friend picked me up from the mall.

The next day, I bought additional clothing and a plane ticket to New York. I knew where to find my homeboys. The cab dropped me off on the block (the place where my friends from Columbus hung out). In twenty minutes, I found one of my friends. We hooked up with two more friends from Columbus.

At this time, the heroin trade was on the decline in New York. There was a new trend emerging. People were free-basing cocaine. We decided to take our heroin and hit the road. We went to Connecticut and opened shop. This state was still an open market for the heroin trade. Connecticut was close enough for us to have some knowledge of the drug culture there. We worked the area for about five months.

When we left Connecticut, we went to Washington D. C. After being there for about a week, we went on to Atlanta. We worked Atlanta for three or four months. This was too close to Columbus. The temptation was too great. I started easing home. I knew my connections in Columbus would make it easy for me to make money. Eventually, I started getting high and stayed in Columbus. Inevitably, I caught another case that sent me back to finish the time I had left on installment. I completed my sentence at another prison, far from home.

In early 1983, I was released on parole. I reported to the parole office only a couple of times. Almost immediately, I started medicating again. After seven months on parole, I was locked up again. There were four months left on the sentence. The parole revocation resulted in my serving the remainder of this time.

After my release in December 1983, I went to Abbeville, Alabama to live for a while. Valerie went with me. We stayed with my relatives. We had kept in contact throughout the years. She had also visited me several times in New York. We stayed there for almost four months. It was hard to find a job in a small town without reliable transportation. I was only able to find a few temporary jobs. Valerie and I were separated before I was locked up. During this time, we were trying to reconcile, but we were still having problems. Inevitably, she went back to Atlanta. One day, she called me and I took a bus to Atlanta.

My uncle (my mother's brother) lived in Atlanta. He agreed to let me stay with him. He had a business manufacturing security doors and windows. He was willing to provide me a temporary job. After a short period, I was able to secure a job with a local construction company. My uncle had a business relationship with them. This job was mentally and physically challenging. This wasn't a problem for me. It provided an avenue for me to get on my feet.

After a couple of weeks, I moved into a boarding house. The house wasn't everything it needed to be. It was in desperate need of repairs. The landlord was reluctant to improve the living arrangements. All of the tenants were preparing to withhold the rent until the repairs were made.

My relationship with Valerie was deteriorating. She was caught up in her own activities and habits. I was unhappy. Things weren't going right for me. The desire to medicate my problems began to tug at me.

The walls of hell were already firmly in place.

With all my Heart

Many waters cannot quench love, neither can the floods drown it: if a man would give all the substance of his house for love, it would utterly be contemned.
Song of Solomon 8:7 (NIV)

When I met Buck, I was vulnerable. I had wanted a good and solid relationship for years. He came along during one of the crisis periods in my life. I met him after years of struggles with other men. I had been battered and bruised from the storm and the rain in my life. Convinced God didn't love me, I walked away from my relationship with Him. Failure was branded across my heart. As a Christian, I had failed. I wanted someone to love me, but I had baggage, and baggage, and baggage.

When we met each other, some of the shallow holes (mild dysfunctions) began to fill, immediately. This led to a need for some serious readjustments. The strain of the adjustment caused the more severe holes (severe dysfunctions) to deepen and widen.

One day, I was at Denna's house sitting on the porch. Denna was a friend of mine. This was where I spent most of my time when I was hanging in the streets. Three guys came up and asked to speak to her inside the house. Two of the guys were familiar to me. However, the third one was unfamiliar. There was something about him capturing my immediate attention, as no one had in years. Our eyes locked on each other. We made a very thorough and complete observation of each other. We didn't say anything with our lips, but our eyes spoke volumes. Man was he fine! After a few minutes in the house, they completed their mission. When they drove off, I asked Denna who he was. She told me his name was Buck. They had stopped by her house to get high. Buck just didn't look the part and it was hard for me to imagine him as a junkie. He was the best-looking man I had seen in a long time.

That night I was planning on going to the H & D in Phenix City with Denna and Jim's sister, Reba. This was very popular club that stayed open late and was always packed. We had all planned to wear red dresses. Jim knew this was our plan. He had another plan. When Denna and I arrived to pick his sister up, my cousin was there with her boyfriend. Reba informed me she wasn't going with us because Jim was planning to take someone else to the same club and she didn't want to be in the middle of our mess. After I assured her there would be no trouble, she agreed to go to the club.

In those days, I was still more of a marijuana smoker or 'Pot Head.' Occasionally, I had snorted small amounts of cocaine, but those could be counted on one hand. At the clubs, I usually drank Coca-Cola. If I felt a need for a buzz, I would go outside and smoke a joint or two. That night, Jim never showed up at the club. However, I was really upset, embarrassed, and hurting. No longer able to hold my feelings inside, I went outside to my car. Once inside the car, I cried like a fool. After all my tears abated, I dried my face. I smoked a joint and returned to the club, ready to move on with the next phase of my life. There was an announcement I needed to make to Reba and Denna. They had heard this before.

"That's the last time he's going to hurt me."

They weren't impressed with my announcement. In spite of their disbelief, this was the last time he was able to inflict pain in my heart. The cycle was broken.

Events began to happen fast inside the club. There were two bars inside the H&D, one when you entered the club and another one in the back of the club. As one of the few bars in the area staying open until 6:00 a.m., it was usually packed. Tonight was no different. Standing near the rear bar, a friend, Pete asked me if I would do him a favor. He had brought a friend with him to the club, but he was leaving the club early. His friend would need a ride home. As he was attempting to introduce me to his friend standing behind me, I turned around. For the second time that day, it happened. My eyes locked with those of this man.

He said, "This is my friend Buck."

I responded, "I'll be more than glad to drop him off."

My heart had been broken, but it was over.

With all my Heart: The Flip Side

Keep thy heart with all diligence; for out of it are the issues of life. Proverbs 4:23

When I met Charlotte, I had been in my own private hell for years. I was looking for a change. In fact, I was praying for a change. My prayer was very specific, "God send someone into my life who has beauty on the inside." My problems were closing in around me. I decided to take a trip to Columbus for the weekend. Maybe the change would be good for me. It had been almost two months since I had seen my mother. The bus ride to Columbus gave me time to think about what I would do when I got there. When I got to Columbus, I could have some fun. The desire to medicate my problems was also closing in on me.

Before leaving Atlanta, I had taken (stolen) some money. While at work, I took the opportunity to steal some money from a local business. This was a technique I had developed as a young boy. I would observe where money was located. At a future date, I would return. If the money was still unsecured, this would provide me the opportunity to steal it. My pockets were fat as I arrived home. My mind was churning. When I arrived at my mother's house, she was glad to see me. She was glad to hear about her brother who also lived in Atlanta. We laughed about all my uncle's rules. He disciplined with an iron fist. He didn't play with his own children. It was nice talking to the family, but I couldn't wait to see my old friends. It didn't take much for me to return to what was familiar, medicating my problems.

It had been almost two years since I had gotten high. Most of the time, I had been in prison. I selected not to get involved in the drug activity there. There was limited access to my drug of choice in prison. I was ready to begin my vicious habit, again. I borrowed my sister's car and went to find my friend, Herb. He had another friend, Ace, with him. Seeing them really enhanced my urge for the drugs. The desire for heroin mixed with cocaine was strong. A 'speedball' seemed to be the ideal solution to my problem. After drinking a beer or two, I was convinced. We headed for a dope house. We put our funds together and bought five or six bags of heroin and some cocaine. We stopped and purchased the works (needles). All we needed was a place to get high. Herb suggested Denna's house.

When we drove into the driveway at the end of the apartment building, there were two young women sitting on Denna's porch. Immediately, I recognized one as Denna. I had known her for several years. However, I didn't recognize the other one. I was on a mission, but I was immediately sidetracked. She was sitting in a dinette chair on the porch. I had never seen her before. Yet, she seemed so familiar. Her legs were wrapped around the legs of the chair. She was wearing blue jeans and a plaid shirt. She seemed to be glowing. As I walked across the porch, I stared into her eyes. She stared back, but we didn't speak. I hadn't been involved with a woman in several months. My eyes traveled slowly over her from head to toe. I felt myself staring. After careful examination, I liked what I saw. I wasn't quick to react.

My friend's voices interrupted my gaze. This was not what we came here for. We were on a different mission. There was something about her I found inviting. This just wasn't the time. I needed to put my thoughts on hold. Drugs were the priority or controlling force. I decided to let it go for temporarily.

Herb asked Denna if we could speak to her inside the apartment. Once inside, she agreed to let us get high and went back to her seat on the porch. Each of us gave her a one-dollar bill. We completed our mission quickly at the kitchen table. They did most of the drugs. It had been a long time since I had gotten high. My system was too vulnerable to consume a larger quantity of the drugs.

When we walked outside again, it was as if time had stood still. She was still sitting there in the same position. Again I stared at her, but I didn't speak. I didn't even nod. The drugs had taken effect. Her eyes were talking to me. They seemed to say she needed a friend. I needed one, too. We needed to talk. With my eyes I tried to communicate this to her. The message I received back said she needed to talk to me. Without saying a word audibly, I walked off.

When we left Denna's place, we went back to Herb's house. His wife was home. This was why we didn't get high at his house. She would have chewed all of us out. I left my sister's car and walked down to the bottom of the hill. There was a package store at the bottom of the hill next to the café. I needed something to drink. For several months, I had been drinking beer. Before I went into the store, I saw Jim. He asked me to get in the car with him. It had been years since we had seen each other. We rode around the block. He told me about his package (drugs). I told him I would get with him later. We had known each other for a long time. We went to Radcliff Elementary together. He was older than I was.

That night, I rode to the H & D with another friend, Pete. He said he was going to leave the club early because he had other plans. These plans didn't interest me. I preferred to remain at the club. He was standing near the bar when he signaled for me to come over.

"I want you to meet someone."

As he was introducing me to his friend, she turned around. I didn't hear the rest of his comments. There she was the woman in red. It was the same young lady I had seen on the porch earlier in the day. I was stunned. The red outfit was made of fine silk. She was wearing red stockings and shoes. There were all kinds of thoughts running through my mind. What was going on? Had Pete set this up? Did she arrange this meeting? Had she conversed with Pete about what had happened between us earlier? I was shocked to see her again. I tried to remain in control of the situation. There was only one thing to do. It was time to talk.

With all my heart, I was ready for a new adventure.

The Dance

Let him kiss me with the kisses of his mouth: for thy love is better than wine. Song of Solomon 1:2

Sure, I was more than willing to give him a ride home. Buck asked me to dance. Normally, I would have said no, but tonight was different. I wanted to dance with this man. The dance floor was packed. I stared into his eyes as we danced and he stared back. When he stared at me, I forgot the pain. I forgot about Jim. In fact, I forgot about everybody on the dance floor and in the club. Truthfully, all that mattered was the warmth flooding my heart when he looked at me with eyes that seemed to pierce my soul. I never looked back at Pete. I was in a different world, a world unfamiliar to me. The magnitude of the attraction was different from anything I had ever felt. His eyes were like magnets. They were magnets that smiled. They beckoned me to come closer. We didn't speak. However, I watched every move of his hands, every move of his feet, but mostly his eyes as we danced. I didn't know if I would ever speak.

After several dances, I returned to my table with my companions. They were still concerned about me. They were drinking alcoholic beverages. My drink of choice was a Coke. Between dances, they continued to watch me. My mind was no longer with them. My eyes kept locking with those of this man across the crowded room. I began to have a fantasy. It wasn't the kind normally coming to mind. We were in a nightclub, but I was having a heavenly vision.

This is what I saw. We were in church. This man was going to be my husband. He was up preaching from the pulpit and I was out in the congregation, dancing in the Spirit. I was near the front of the church. God was actually far from my mind. When I was attending church, I had never danced in the Spirit. Marriage wasn't on my mind. I was so shocked by this that I told him. He simply responded several people had prophesied to him that he was going to be a preacher. My companions never noticed the sparks firing between this man who I had just met and me.

As we drove from the club, Reba sat in the front seat. She was worn out and dropping off to sleep. Denna sat in the back seat with Buck making passes at him. It never occurred to her that I was interested in him. Buck remained quiet. He gave no indication he heard her. He was sitting directly behind me. In the rear view mirror, I kept looking at him and he kept looking at me. We stopped to get something to eat and ran into two other people we knew. They were looking for something to do and told Denna they would come by her house. Reba wanted to go home and I was relieved. She didn't need to be with me for the rest of this night.

When everybody arrived at Denna's, the party continued and so did this gaze between Buck and me. We weren't talking with our mouths; our eyes were saying enough. It must have been hours that this communication continued between us. At least, it seemed this way.

Wherein times past ye walked according to the course of this world, according to the prince and power of the air, the spirit that worketh in the children of disobedience:

Among whom also we had our conversations in times past in the lust of our flesh, fulfilling the desires of the flesh and the mind; and were by nature the children of wrath, even as others.
Ephesians 2:2-3

There was a saucer filled with cocaine and there was plenty of marijuana. The party continued, but our efforts to get high weren't working. We were both distracted by the chemistry, not the chemistry of the drugs, but an internal chemistry. We had barely spoken ten words since we met. No one seemed to notice. Our eyes were speaking volumes to each other. His eyes said, "I know you." However, this wasn't possible. Surely, I would have remembered meeting him. There was a private conversation going on and we were getting to know each other.

Finally, Buck broke the silence and asked me if I wanted to talk to him. We excused ourselves to one of the bedrooms. Conversation came easy for us. We talked about everything. At this point, we were two strangers exchanging the most intimate details of our life stories. It seemed he had always been a part of my life. It was amazing we had journeyed through all the same cities at opposite times. We knew most of the same people from the streets, but our paths had never crossed.

After we talked for a while (hours), he asked me to move next to him on the bed. Since we entered the bedroom, I had been sitting in a chair near the bed. I explained to him I didn't believe in one-night stands. If anything were ever going to happen between us, he would have to be ready for a long-term commitment. A strange thing to tell a stranger, yet, even stranger, he agreed to this stipulation. He told me what I wanted to hear.

At this time, I was extremely self-conscious of my body, which made everything happening even stranger. Whether, it was winter or summer, I always wore turtleneck dickeys and long sleeves. My scars were confined to places that could be almost completely hidden by my clothes. This was my sign to the world. I didn't want to be asked about the scars. My mother was still the only person who knew what had happened to me on the burning bed. There was now a second person who knew the story.

What you have said in the dark will be heard in the daylight, and what you have whispered in the ear in the inner rooms will be proclaimed from the roofs. Luke 12:3 (NIV)

When daylight found us still together, I was shocked by my actions. It was at this time I remembered Jim. It was almost noon. He would be looking for me soon. Denna's house would be his first stop. I was finished with the relationship, but I wasn't ready for an unnecessary conflict. I wanted to hurry home. More accurately, I wanted to leave Denna's house as quickly as possible.

When we left the apartment, we left Denna asleep. Buck's mother lived a few blocks away. The drive ended too quickly. We agreed we would meet at the H & D again that night. After dropping him off, I headed home.

All day he remained on my mind and I wanted to see him again. It had been only a few hours since I had dropped him off, but it seemed like such a long time. I didn't want to wait until nightfall. Denna and I decided to head to Ninth Street. Maybe, I would see him there. I had never hung out in this area of Wynnton. Usually, when I came through there with Jim, I remained in the car. When we arrived, Jim and Reba were on Ninth Street. He was flirting with everybody, as usual. They were sitting on the porch of a house across from Jack Marshall's Cafe. We joined the crowd sitting there. Next to the house, there was a group of people selling drugs. I wasn't interested in anything going on around me.

Patiently, I waited until I saw the vision I had been anticipating. It wasn't long before I got my wish. My memory of him walking down the street is still vividly embedded in my memory. Buck was tall, dark, handsome, and fine. He strolled leisurely down the street. There was something in his walk almost defining his personality. His walk said he had no worries, no cares, or concerns. He was very neatly groomed, wearing a plaid shirt and blue jeans were starched to perfection. His soft leather boots matched the dominant color in his shirt, gray.

As he stopped near the place I was sitting, he engaged in a brief conversation. As he was talking, he found my eyes. He knew Jim was sitting there, but he signaled for me to come towards him. It didn't matter to me that Jim was there. I walked over to him at the edge of the curb. We confirmed our date for that night. When he walked back up the streets, my eyes followed him. Still, no one noticed I was acting totally out of character. A week before, there was no way I would have engaged in a private conversation with a man in front of Jim, nor would I have stayed on Ninth Street for more than a few minutes.

Before going to the club that night, Denna and I stopped on Ninth Street. Jim was there and we had a brief confrontation inside the café. He took the keys to my car and drove off. A few feet away, Buck was playing pool. I asked Denna to explain to Buck what was going on. When Jim returned about thirty minutes later, he gave me the keys to the car and walked away. He never looked back. Buck rode with me to the club. As we walked out of the café and got into my car, it appeared no one noticed a man getting into the car with me.

After we left the club, Buck went home with me. We spent the next day together. He had planned to take the bus back to Atlanta on Sunday afternoon. This is where he was living and working. He planned on returning to Columbus the following Friday. Needless to say, he missed the bus. It wasn't long before I took him to meet my mother and children. That night, I drove him back to Atlanta. He was concerned about me driving back to Columbus alone. He asked one of his friends, Willie, to ride to Atlanta with us. I didn't know Willie.

The next day, Willie told Jim about my trip to Atlanta and my new relationship with Buck. This led to another minor confrontation between Jim and me. After the confrontation with Jim, Denna and I drove around the street to her sister's house. Willie was there, getting high. For his information, Jim had given him a sack of dope.

In spite of all this, Jim assumed this was something that would pass and he was still in control. He was wrong, I had cried him out of my system and my thoughts were focused on Buck. Within a few days, I had another confrontation with Jim. Nothing was going to hinder my weekend, including Jim. I was expecting Buck to come back to see me on the next evening.

The Dance: The Flip Side

Thou art all fair, my love; there is no spot in thee.
Song of Solomon 4:7

This moment had been building all day. I asked her to dance and she agreed. She didn't say anything. She smiled and nodded her head. As we danced, we continued to stare at each other. There was a song playing, "Take these shackles off my feet so I can dance." It really described how I felt, free. I felt alive and excited. There were two reasons I felt free. I was free of prison and a bad relationship. There were so many feelings inside of me. There were so many unanswered questions. There were so many things I wanted to know. I wanted to know everything about her. What was going on? Was it a setup? Did Pete plan this with her? I knew I had prayed to God. Was this the answer to my prayer? Had He answered my prayer so quickly? I wasn't living my life for Him, but I knew He had the power to help me.

After the first dance, there was another dance and another. When I held her in my arms, I felt she belonged to me. I was in control. Normally, slow dancing wasn't something I did. I preferred trying to look cool. When I finally came off the dance floor, one of my friends remarked I had tried to dance every dance. We walked outside to his BMW. Inside the car, we sniffed cocaine. Sniffing wasn't my preference, but I did it to be social.

When I came back in the club, I stopped at the bar for a drink. I began trying to make my way back to where she was sitting. Another friend stopped me. We talked for a moment. Finally, I made my way back across the room and was able to get her back on the dance floor. The dance floor was crowded, but it allowed us some privacy away from our friends.

As we were dancing, she told me about a vision. She told me she saw me in the pulpit preaching. She also told me I was going to be her husband. It wasn't anything new. In the past, I had been told I was going to be a preacher. The rest remained to be seen. My prayer was still on my mind. For some unexplained reason, I wasn't overwhelmed or disturbed by what she said.

> *Do not set foot on the path of the wicked or walk in the way of evil men. Avoid it, do not travel on it; turn from it and go on your way. For they cannot sleep till they do evil; they are robbed of slumber till they make someone fall. They eat the bread of wickedness and drink the wine of violence.* Proverbs 4:14-17

At the end of the evening, we walked outside the club. We didn't talk. When we made our way to the car, the car looked familiar. Sitting in the back seat of the car, I continued to wonder if it was a conspiracy. Denna was being Denna. She wasn't on my mind. It was easy to tune her out. She was trying to get something going. This was to no avail. The lady in red was vividly on my mind.

We dropped Reba off at home. Afterwards, we stopped by a nearby restaurant and ordered breakfast to go. We ran into two friends. As we were leaving the restaurant, they had a fistfight with a guy in the parking lot. It was over a parking space. The guy came out on the losing end. He sped off without getting anything to eat. One of my friends said he was coming over to Denna's house. As we were riding down the street, I told Charlotte

I was going to Denna's. I wasn't ready to be dropped off. I wasn't ready for the night to end.

Until the day break, and the shadows flee
away, I will get me to the mountain of myrrh,
and to the hill of frankincense...
Song of Solomon 4:6

We all arrived at the house about the same time. We got high for a couple of hours. One of the guys left early. Afterwards, I asked Charlotte to come to the backroom. We dismissed ourselves and went into the bedroom to talk. There were twin beds in the room and a chair. The room was crowded. The easiest place for me to sit was on the bed. We started talking, and talking, and talking. I asked about her car. She told me about Jim. Earlier in the day, I had ridden in the same car with him. Everything happening that day seemed strangely connected to her.

We talked for a couple of hours. There were so many things I wanted to ask her. The more questions I asked her, the more I wanted to ask. What year was she here? Who did she meet? Who did she know? Why hadn't I met her before? Why hadn't I met her sooner? How could we know so many of the same people and not know each other? It seemed like an impossibility we hadn't met before this day. There were so many common events we shared. The more we talked, the more I was amazed. We shared our secrets, hurts, and disappointments. I became more relaxed. We talked about failed and failing relationships. I wanted to know her better.

After we talked, I wanted her to move closer to me. I needed her to feel safe and protected. It was important for her to feel comfortable with me, to know the kind of guy I was. She was hesitant, but eventually, she moved near me. We laughed for some time. I enjoyed seeing her laugh. I told her what I needed to tell her to make her comfortable with me. It was more of a challenge for me. In the back of my mind, I thought we were going to be just friends. I needed a friend. Beyond this, I had no plans for a future with her.

Before ending our time together, I wanted to hold her again. There wasn't time. She was in a hurry to leave. When we left the apartment, Denna was asleep in the other bedroom with my friend. Charlotte dropped me off at my mother's house. We made plans to meet that night at the H & D. As she drove off, I thought "that's someone I want to know better."

After changing clothes, I went back to Herb's house. That afternoon, I walked down the street to the package store. As the lady was bagging my purchase, I was startled by the view of five to seven ladies across the street sitting on a porch. One face stood out from the crowd of women. She looked as if she didn't belong. Nevertheless, in the streets, a decent face can fool you. Yet, in this face something was very sweet and different. I made my way across the street. I signaled to the woman who was so appealing to my taste. I told her I wanted to see her that night. At this time, I was headed back to Herb's house. Charlotte nodded her head in agreement. I knew I would see her that evening. Excitement overwhelmed me. I looked forward to the evening.

That evening, I walked down Ninth Street to the café. There were pool tables near the bar in Jack Marshall's. Pool was another game in which I was skilled. I was into my game and didn't notice when she walked into the café. After a few games, Denna came over and explained what was going on between Charlotte and Jim. I didn't notice the confrontation.

When he brought the car back, we headed for the club. We took a table at the back of the room. This night we spent less time on the dance floor. Whenever Denna was dancing, we had time to talk. However, whenever certain songs came on, we headed for the dance floor. At the end of the evening, we dropped Denna off at home. Actually, it was morning when the club closed. After dropping Denna off, we drove across town to Charlotte's house.

I was scheduled to take the bus back to Atlanta Sunday afternoon. Normally, I don't talk a lot to strangers. However, there was something about her that made me relax. Her conversation kept me talking. I continued asking questions. I was aiming to know the inner person. The day seemed to end too quickly. My mother didn't see me until it was time for me to pick my clothes up. I missed the last bus to Atlanta for the day. The next morning, I was scheduled to be at work. I needed to be back in Atlanta, as soon as possible. Charlotte offered to drive me back. This was the best solution. It allowed us more time together.

It was getting late when we prepared to leave. It was going to be near midnight when she returned from Atlanta. We picked up her children from her mother's house. After I filled the car with gas, I wanted someone to ride with us. I didn't want her driving back to Columbus alone. It was too dangerous for her to be alone with her children on the highway at night.

We went through Ninth Street. As we were driving down the street, I saw Willie. He was someone I had known for years. I asked him to ride to Atlanta with us. It wasn't that I trusted him. He owed me a favor. It would also give me a chance to test her before our relationship went any further. If she was a weak woman, someone would tell me what had happened between them. Wynnton was known for keeping rumors going. I was counting on this working in my favor. It was better for me to know what I was dealing with before the relationship went any further. If he tried to get next to her, she would tell me. That is if she was the right woman for me. I would straighten him if he tried anything with her.

You, my brothers, were called to be free. But do not use your freedom to indulge the sinful nature rather, serve one another in love.
Galatians 5:13

When we arrived at my room, I gave Herman some potato chips. He wasted the chips everywhere. Shortly after our arrival, a girl across the hall went to buy some reefer for us. After we smoked a few joints, I put Charlotte back on the road. It was getting late. Earline had to attend school the next morning. I had to work.

Before she left, I promised to see her again on Friday. Mother's Day was coming up on Sunday. I wanted to be there for my mother. I had already given her a present, but I wanted to have dinner with her. Now, I had another reason to come back. I felt free in more than one way. The shackles were off my feet!

The Move

By night on my bed I sought him whom my soul loveth: I sought him, but I found him not. I will rise now, and go about the city in the streets, and in the broad ways I will seek him whom my soul loveth: I sought him, but I found him not. Song of Solomon 3:1-2 (NIV)

All week, I had made plans for a romantic weekend with Buck. Well, when Friday came, the steaks were marinating and the champagne was chilling. As the evening progressed, there was one problem. There was no Buck. He didn't have a telephone, so I couldn't call him. I waited for him all night. My telephone never rang.

Early Saturday morning, I drove to Atlanta to clarify the future of our relationship. I arrived at his apartment building before 10:00 a.m. The previous weekend, he had introduced me to one of his neighbors. Rather than knocking on his door this early in the morning, I decided it would be better if she told him I was in town. I gave her a note to give him with a number where I could be reached in Atlanta. As she knocked on the door, I waited in the hall for his response. After she gave him the message, he looked down the hall. He looked directly at me. Trying to hide his shock, he asked me into his apartment. I only had one question.

"Are you glad to see me?"

He responded, "I'm shocked, but I'm glad."

Within a few minutes, he started packing his clothes for Columbus. The next time he returned to Atlanta, it would be to pick up the rest of his belongings, completing his move to Columbus. That was almost twenty years ago.

The following day was Mother's Day. His family was planning a big family dinner. He took us (the children and me) to the dinner at his sister's house. It was a huge meal, barbecue ribs, steaks, and chicken with all the trimmings. I took beef ribs for Buck because he didn't eat pork. I had already learned a lot about him. This included the fact he had a healthy appetite. When I prepared his plate or should I say plates, I prepared him two plates at once. One plate contained meat and bread. The second plate was loaded with vegetables. Everyone was watching to see if I had given him too much food. He devoured both plates and dessert.

After dinner, Buck told me he was going to run an errand. He said he would be gone for only a few minutes. After he was gone for more than an hour, I became concerned. I expressed my concern to one of his sisters.

"He's been gone for a long time."

"As long as you have been knowing him, you should have known it was going to be more than a few minutes."

"How long do you think I have known him?"

"Years!"

"I just met him last week."

"I don't believe it. It doesn't seem like it."

It didn't seem like it to me. It felt like years.

The Move: The Flip Side

Also I will ordain a place for My people Israel, and will plant them, and they shall dwell in their place, and shall be moved no more; neither shall the children of wickedness waste them any more, as at the beginning,
1 Chronicles 17:9

Saturday morning, I heard a knock on the boarding house door. I was the newest person living in the house. As you entered the front door, my room was the first door on the right. Being new, I assumed the visitor was looking for someone else. Directly across from my room, there was another room. Tanya lived in that room. I had introduced her to Charlotte the previous Sunday. There was a knock on my door. I pulled on my bathrobe before answering the door. It was Tanya.

"Buck, somebody is out here looking for you."

I peeped out of the door of my room in total amazement. Charlotte was standing down the hall. She stood there slightly smiling. I asked her into my room. I wondered if someone had told her I needed a ride. We had a date for the previous evening, but I wasn't able to make it. My intentions were never to stand her up. She made only one remark.

"Are you glad to see me?"

"Yes."

My response was "yes." Nevertheless, I hadn't expected to see her so soon. This gave me an opportunity to do the things hindering my trip. My paycheck needed to be picked up and I needed to pick up my clothes at the dry cleaners. I explained to her why I hadn't been able to make it to Columbus.

There were so many problems with the boarding house. I was ready to move. Immediately, I began packing my clothes. As I packed, we talked about our previous weekend. We talked about what had been good. We also talked about things that could be better. She told me about the confrontation with Jim. He was reluctant to let her walk out of his life. I had known Jim for a long time. This situation could be resolved without an unnecessary conflict. I wasn't going to back away from the relationship.

After we took care of the loose ends in Atlanta, we headed to Columbus. We never really discussed the next step in our relationship. When we arrived, we went to her apartment. We unpacked the car as if it was understood; I was moving in with her. I was supposed to be visiting for a week.

Things were moving fast between us. Whatever my original thoughts were about our relationship, they were changing quickly. She did more than smile at me. In the beginning, it seemed she catered to me. There was another side of her I didn't know. Her showing up on my doorstep should have been an indication, but I didn't catch the hint. She was a very determined, willful, and strong spirited woman. Additionally, she was full of surprises. It was hard to be bored around her. She kept me entertained and laughing. As the relationship progressed, I would learn she had a lot of nerve.

I called my mother to let her know I was in town. I also informed her I would be bringing guests home for dinner. My sister was barbecuing and everybody was bringing a covered dish. I didn't eat pork. When we arrived at my sister's house with the children, we brought chicken, steaks, and beef ribs. My mother lived next door to my sister. When Charlotte prepared my food, she used two plates. One plate was loaded with meat and bread. The other plate contained a variety of vegetables. Afterwards, she gave me another plate with a variety of desserts.

One of my sisters commented about how long I had been involved with Charlotte. She was sure it had been going on a long time. I thought she had heard something on the street. I told her it had been a week. She thought I was lying. It was hard to hide the comfort we felt with each other. I was comfortable with the children, too. They were comfortable with me.

After I was sure they were comfortable with my family, I decided to leave for a short break. Ninth Street was calling me. The monkey I had awakened was calling me. Telling her I would be back in a few minutes, I went to get me some dope. It took me longer than I planned. When I returned, I offered an explanation for the delay.

At the end of the week, I was enjoying my new relationship. She told me I could stay in Columbus. This was appealing to me. We went back to Atlanta to pickup the rest of my belongings. I was moving in. It wouldn't be a one-night stand or a weekend fling.

True Partners

Don't be fooled by those who try to excuse these sins, for the terrible anger of God comes upon all those who disobey him. Don't participate in the things these people do. For though your hearts were once full of darkness, now you are full of light from the Lord, and your behavior should show it! Ephesians 5:6-8 (NLT)

Mama wasn't happy about any of this, with the exception of my ending the relationship with Robert. She was constantly concerned about what I was doing. For me, this was hard to understand. Why wouldn't she accept the way I had decided to live my life? In my efforts to respect my mother, I always tried to keep my illegal activities away from her. During the time I had been struggling with the issues in the marriage, she was new in her walk with the Lord. She had been very careful about advising me, not wanting to give me the wrong advice. This was going to change when I picked up my new habits. She began to dream about these habits and she wasn't about to reserve her opinions.

There had been times when I was in New York that I had picked pockets or taken advantage of someone. However, for the most part this wasn't my hustle. Sometimes, a Good Samaritan passing by the scene would intervene. This happened on one occasion when we had walked off with a man's wallet. It happened near Wall Street. A Good Samaritan walked up on us and made us give the wallet back to the man. We had walked away without the man missing his wallet.

I was involved with another kind of thief, a real thief. It wouldn't be long before I would pick up this new habit. Shopping was what I did best and shoplifting was what he did best. Five minutes in a store and I could spot the most expensive items into the store. This would be my new job, spotting the items, or moving them all to one location in the store. This earned me a cut of the profits and one of each outfit. By one of each outfit, I mean I wanted one in every color and each style. The other people on the team took turns removing the items from the store. Buck's favorite thing was trashing the stores. By this process, he was able to lift all of the clothes from the rack with one swift movement and with the precision of a surgeon, roll the items together, placing them in a garbage bag. After he made his way to the outside of the store, he carried the bag as if he was a store employee taking out the trash.

But he, being full of compassion, forgave
their iniquity, and destroyed them not: yea,
many a time turned He his anger away, and
did not stir up all His wrath. Psalm 78:38

Buck had a drug addiction driving his stealing. Mine was an addiction to clothes. I drank champagne everyday and smoked marijuana as if it was a cigarette. When I purchased the marijuana, I would clean the seeds from all of it, roll all of it, and place the joints in a box next to my bed. There were always joints next to my bed. After all, I was constantly smoking one joint behind the other. I was looking for something I didn't have. I wanted to be happy and marijuana made me laugh. This didn't make me happy, but laughing was a close second.

Mama began to call me, warning me to stop the things I was doing. She told me God had shown her what I was doing. To avoid disrespecting her, I would lay the telephone down. Occasionally, I would pick up the telephone to see if she was still talking. Periodically, I would make a very brief comment, "Uh huh." This was just to make her think I was listening to her. She continued trying to warn me, but I wasn't listening. She continued to call every single night, with her warnings. This was to no avail, since most of the time the telephone was lying on the bed.

Every day, we dressed to go to work, wearing expensive clothes. Each night, we planned where we would be working the next day, stealing. We would travel out of town to steal. The pay was excellent, our parts averaging five hundred to a thousand dollars a day. The hours weren't bad either. The stress was horrible; I was constantly worrying we would be caught. This feeling usually came on after we left the store. I was never scared in the process of committing the crimes. The panic hit me, after we left the stores. However, by the next morning, the fear would be gone. Usually, by noon each day, we had enough goods to reach our daily quota.

A couple of months into the relationship, we were arrested and charged with approximately twelve counts of shoplifting. This is an approximation because after we were released on bond, the police continued to add on additional charges. When we were arrested, we didn't have any merchandise on us. The owner of one of the shops had identified us as stealing something from his store. The police decide to detain us, mostly because they knew Buck's reputation. They placed a hold on us to prevent us from making bond. That evening, the police found an abandoned car downtown. The car was registered to me.

The car was full of items we had accumulated over several days. Through a process, which could only be called "guesswork," they attempted to identify where these items came from. There were no identifying labels on any of the items. We were charged with even stealing items we had purchased. This went on for two days and finally my lawyer was able to get the holds dropped. Once I was released on bond, I arranged for Buck's release. Frustrated with trying to identify one of the more costly items, a pair of brass bookends with a marble base, the detectives agreed to stop searching for charges, if I would tell them where these came from. To stop the process, I provided the information.

All of the charges were eventually lumped together for the plea bargain. Buck claimed responsibility for the crimes. Subsequently, he was sentenced to prison and I was placed on probation.

Since Buck had confessed to the charges, I felt obligated to support him financially and physically during his incarceration. This meant I was going to support him by sending him money orders regularly and visiting him at least once a week. Buck was sent to Hardwick, Georgia after he completed diagnostic assessment in Jackson, Georgia. Visitation there required you talk through a huge metal screen resembling the screen on a barbecue pit, just in exaggerated proportions. While he was incarcerated at Jackson, I only visited him once.

Hardwick, Georgia was approximately thirty miles from Macon. You were only allowed to visit on a Saturday or a Sunday, not both days. It had been a long time since I had spent any real time with Buck and I wanted to see him both days. I came up with a plan to fulfill this desire. That weekend, I rented a room at a local motel for the night. Saturday, I arrived at the prison wearing a wig and sunglasses. In my hand was Buck's sister's birth certificate. My plan included using her name the first day in case my plot was spoiled on the second day. Additionally, I changed my handwriting when I signed in under her name. The first day came off without a hitch. The next day, I arrived without the wig and sunglasses, as myself. Shortly after visitation began, the guards asked me to come outside the visiting room. They asked me if I had visited Buck the day before. Assuring them I hadn't, I asked them to check the sign-in roster and to compare the names and signatures. Knowing they remembered Buck kissing the other woman, I explained she probably had been drinking and this made her overly affectionate. Not being able to prove otherwise, they let me return to visitation.

A huge fence surrounded Rivers Correctional Facility. Inside the fence, the prison was separated into four separate buildings, each having their own separate visitation room. The seats in the room resembled church pews. One guard was stationed at the front of the visitation room. The other officers remained outside during most of the visitation period. Since I was visiting each Saturday, some of the guards knew me by name. I was observing them, too. Believing there was corruption in everything, I was waiting to catch them slipping on the job and catch them I would.

One Saturday, one of the officers was struggling to stay awake. This went on throughout the visitation period of about five hours. To make sure the officer knew I had caught him sleeping, I winked at him. I nicknamed him Sleepy, but I was careful to assure Buck was the only person who knew what I had on him.

Whenever I went to see Buck, I always carried money. One day when I went to see Buck, I was the only visitor in this visitation room and Sleepy was working visitation. He kept walking out of the room leaving us alone. Buck was scared for me to ask him, but Sleepy was in my debt. Against Buck's protests, I called Sleepy over and made him a proposition. I told him if he left us alone for the rest of the visitation period, I would give him twenty dollars. Sleepy said he didn't want the money, but he agreed to leave the room for the remainder of our visit. When I walked out the fence after visitation, I heard someone calling my name.

"Charlotte, Charlotte."

I turned to see two guards peeping from a window; one was Sleepy.

"Come back inside the gate."

When I walked back down the sidewalk, Sleepy said, "Drop that on the ground by my car."

He described his car. As I walked back through the gate headed towards the parking lot, I laughed. I had been right, I was sure the corruption existed. I dropped the twenty dollars on the ground by his car.

Things turned sour at Rivers, one Saturday when I went to see Buck. When I pulled up, some of the prisoners were in the windows; they were trying to signal something was wrong inside the prison by hollering 'raisin bread.' When I got inside, a female guard said she would have to search another female visitor and me. As I had nothing on me, except $170, I agreed to the search. She was checking for drugs and I didn't have any on me.

There were ways to get drugs into the prison. Me walking in with drugs wasn't one of the options. After the search, she asked me to take the money back to the car before proceeding to visitation. I told her I needed to get my keys from someone riding with me. Actually, I needed to warn one my riders. She was visiting someone in one of the other buildings. She was taking him marijuana. It had nothing to do with Buck or me.

When I left the prison, I was still angry about how I had been treated. My rider hadn't been searched. Monday, I reported the incident to the warden at the prison. He told me he had received a report about this incident. The report stated I arrived at the prison with $770 on me. He further stated they suspected I was bringing this money to Buck for him to purchase drugs. When I asked him why I had been allowed to visit if this was the allegation, he couldn't provide me with an answer. He also informed me I would no longer be allowed to visit Buck. There was no way I was going to be deterred by this action. After I finished talking to him, I began arranging for Buck to be transferred. Within two weeks, he was transferred to Jack Rutledge State Prison in Columbus. At least, I would no longer have to make the long trips.

For they heard an awesome trumpet blast
and a voice and a message so terrible that
they begged God to stop speaking.
Hebrews 12:19 (NLT)

Shortly after Buck went to prison, I went back to selling drugs. The incident at the prison didn't pressure me to close my business. The drug business was going good, until Mama started dreaming again. I was starting to resent these dreams exposing everything I was trying to hide from her. She called me one night and told me she had dreamed I was selling drugs. I assured her she was severely mistaken. There was no way I would ever stoop to selling drugs. She insisted on telling me if I didn't stop what I was doing, I was going to be caught. This warning was familiar to me. This was the same warning she gave me when I was stealing. This time she was resolutely determined to acquire and maintain my undivided attention.

"We both had dreams," they answered, "but there is no one to interpret them." Then Joseph said to them, "Do not interpretations belong to God? Tell me your dreams." Genesis 40:8 (NIV)

She said, "The police were searching your house. They were tearing your sofa apart. It was as if, they were sure you had the dope in the sofa. They were tearing the foam in the back of the sofa into small pieces."

While I was assuring her I would never stoop to selling drugs, at the same time, I was down on my knees in front of the sofa. The telephone was in my left hand and my right hand was reaching into the back of the sofa. I was pulling the marijuana from my hiding place, the hiding place no one knew about, except God. All I wanted was for her to hurry up and get off the telephone. She repeated her warnings several times, describing each detail of her dream.

She continued explaining, repeatedly, "The police were searching your house for drugs. They were so sure you had the drugs they were ripping your sofa to pieces. They were ripping the foam into small pieces."

I was trying to remain calm, but I was afraid the police would get there before she hung up the telephone. Mama never said anything important only once. If something were really pressing on her mind, she would repeat the message until she got tired. I needed to get the dope out of the house before the police arrived. Finally, she was finished. Nervously, I placed the drugs in a jar, rushed out of the house and quickly buried the drugs in the ground.

Surely the Lord God will do nothing, but He revealeth His secret unto His servants the prophets. Amos 3:7

All night long, I stayed awake, expecting the police to show up. For a few days, I was scared to sell anything. Then, the devil gave me another plan. He talked to me real good and based on everything that had happened in the past, I was convinced he was right. He told me before anything happened to me, God would warn my mother and she would warn me. All I had to do was find a new place to sell the drugs and avoid talking to my mother. As long as she was unable to talk to me, nothing would happen. This would keep me from getting caught selling drugs. This was a perfect plan.

Two weeks after her warning, I went to see Denna. Almost immediately, I set up shop at her apartment. In addition to splitting the profits with her, I was also giving her part of the drugs for recreational use. All of this resulted because I was afraid to talk to my mother.

My plan was working. Mama hadn't been able to reach me by telephone for some time. Business was going extremely well. All of my bills were paid off and I was doing plenty of shopping. I was able to buy my children anything and everything they wanted. Every day, I smoked as much marijuana as I wanted. Only now, I sprinkled cocaine in my joints. This is called lacing. Sometimes I snorted cocaine, but more than that I liked licking the bags containing the cocaine.

She obeyed not the voice; she received not correction; she trusted not in the Lord; she drew not near to her God. Zephaniah 3:2

There was only one problem with my thriving business. At this point, 'Something' began to talk to me, regularly. I called God 'Something.' The voice constantly said, "You're going to get caught." Whenever, I told anybody what the voice said, they told me I was just paranoid because I had been snorting too much cocaine. The voice became more frequent and more insistent.

"You're going to get caught."

There was no doubt in my mind where the voice was coming from, but I wasn't going to admit I knew the source.

Finally, I told Denna I was going to stop selling drugs. The fear of being caught with the drugs had become overwhelming. Denna told me she had several bills that hadn't been paid for the month. I agreed to get one more package to help her out of the financial strain. This was a mistake. The last package changed my life. It also severed our friendship.

I was breaking down the drugs when I heard the voice of 'Something' speak again. This time I knew I wasn't paranoid.

He said, "The police are in the house."

There was no doubt in my mind what was happening inside the house.

True Partners: The Flip Side

It is of the LORD's mercies that we are not consumed,
because His compassions fail not... Lamentations 3:22

It wasn't long before my addiction flared up full force. Each day, I would use Charlotte's car to go stealing with my friends. I would leave her waiting for my return. After I scored, I would pick her up to help me sell the merchandise. One day, I went to take off a lick (steal something from a location I had scouted previously). She was waiting for me on Ninth Street. The guys with me were scared to go through with it. I was determined to complete the mission. I knew someone who had the heart to help me.

"Man, let me go get my woman."

We went back to Ninth Street and I told her what I had in mind. Just as I thought, she was game to help me pull it off. It went off without a hitch. This changed the way we did business. From then on, she was going with me. If it was a heavy job, she was the driver to aid our escape. If it was clothing, she picked and organized the outfits.

The first lick I took her on became one of my favorite spots. We were burning it up. We would park in a parking lot adjacent to the business. She remained in the car with it running. When we threw the tires across the fence, she would help us load the car. One day, we jumped the fence and sneaked inside the warehouse. Once inside, Lee was hesitating. One of the employees spotted Lee turning the corner. We ran and jumped the fence. I ran past the car where Charlotte was waiting. Lee and Ace ran towards the car, but I told them to keep running. Charlotte picked us up around the corner. The man was watching from the other side of the fence.

We drove back to Wynnton. We were driving down the street when Ace saw one of his friends. The guy asked us for a ride. He rode with us for approximately three blocks. When we turned on Ninth Street, the police were there. They were looking for the car. They spotted it, as I was parking. I jumped out and walked away fast. I went inside a friend's apartment. Ace and his friend got out of the car. Charlotte slid over into the driver's seat. Lee wasn't with us. We had dropped him off around the street. The policemen pulled guns on Ace and his friend. They forced them to lie on the ground face down. Charlotte was asked to step outside the car. She left her pocketbook in the car. The police officer removed it from the car. When he searched the pocketbook, there was a gun inside. They were all taken back to the store to be identified. The strange thing was the man could only positively identify one person. The person he identified was the wrong person. Ace's friend, the only person who hadn't been in the area was positively identified.

They were arrested and taken downtown. The store had received a shipment of tires that day. Four of the tires were missing. We didn't take them. When Charlotte was released on bond, she went back to talk to the owner of the business. She convinced him to drop the charges against her. They were also dropped against Ace. However, the person who was totally in the dark about the tires was sentenced on the charge. Afterwards, he told me, he learned a valuable lesson. He would never be quick to jump into a car again.

Charlotte loved clothes. She was sure her needs were considered in every bag. Sometimes, my partners got upset because she wanted so many outfits. In the end, she got every outfit she wanted. She also had to have shoes and stockings to match each outfit. I nicknamed her, 'Sporty O'tee.' She wore a new outfit every day. It was good advertisement for my business. If she wore it, others wanted it. Dressing in this fashion made it easy to steal. She looked rich. It was also easy for her to converse with store employees.

Money was rolling into the house. This gave us a double cut on the ventures involving other people. Drugs consumed most of my money. She smoked reefer and drank champagne. However, she made sure everything at the house was covered. One day each month was used to supply the house with food, toiletries, and clothes for the kids. We also stole the other necessities. We took one day a month to earn the money to pay the household bills. We hired babysitters to watch the kids and paid them well. At night, we planned for the next day.

My relatives couldn't understand what was going on between us. Some of them tried to get me back with Valerie. Charlotte's mother was also trying to figure it out. She would call at night. Charlotte would hold the telephone to my ear to allow me to hear the conversation. She was providing the right message, but we weren't listening. Our minds were far from any advice she offered. We were caught up in the lifestyle. The drugs put any remorse on hold.

I took Charlotte to a revival tent meeting one night. At this service we found nothing to make us consider repenting for our lifestyle. In fact, we saw many things reminding us of the confidence games we saw in the streets. In the end, we discussed what we saw. At the time, we thought it was funny. Today, we find it sad.

We began to make bigger plans for stealing. Sometimes, it seemed we were running out of places to hit. My habit was getting worse. It was requiring greater quantities of drugs to prevent me from becoming sick. We often had to make a quick run to get the monkey (withdrawals) off my back. A small lick in the mornings would give me enough money to cop (purchase) enough drugs to ease my sickness. Once the initial sickness was over, we could hit the highway.

One day as we were doing one of these quick hits, things went wrong. We did only limited stealing in Columbus. We seldom went downtown to steal. The kind of merchandise we were moving wasn't readily available there. This day, we hit several stores downtown. Before long, we were stopped. We saw the policeman coming and we were able to hide the merchandise we were carrying. Since we didn't have anything on us, we didn't expect anything to come out of it. The storeowner made a positive identification. We were taken to the jail. No merchandise had been found. Little did we know that a few days earlier, we had been implicated at another store. Charlotte was wearing one of the dresses from the store. They didn't recognize the dress. The next day, she had to go to court in the dress. She told me she was wearing the evidence. Someone from the store came down to identify us, but they didn't notice the outfit.

The first day, it seemed as if they questioned us for hours. One of the detectives was familiar with me. I didn't know him. He was nasty and tried to scare us.

"So you're the Henry Buckwheat Johnson."

"Do I know you?"

"No! But before this is over, you will."

He also thought he was smart. He kept trying to bluff us into talking, but everything he said was wrong. At the end of the day, they found the car. It was packed with excess merchandise we had been unable to sell. Then, there came the challenge of trying to identify the merchandise. This was the joke. The name of the stores had been removed from most of the merchandise. Rather than detective work, it turned into a guessing game. The merchandise and charges were confused. It was as if somebody pulled the name of a store out of a hat and said the merchandise belonged to that store. In the end, it didn't matter. With my record, I would have to enter a plea bargain.

After several days, we were allowed to make bond. They had prevented us from making bond to allow them time to identify the merchandise. My addiction had worn off. When we were released, we went back to work. We needed money to pay a lawyer and the bondsman. There was one stipulation; we didn't mess with Columbus. We were sure almost every store in the city had been shown our pictures. We put the show on the road. The addiction was soon back.

To complicate matters, things became strained between Charlotte and me. Valerie came to town. Some members of my family were pressuring me to reconcile with her. Since we had these cases, Charlotte wasn't going away. I felt pulled in several directions. The decision was taken out of my hands when I was locked back up.

Valerie came to see me at the jail. We talked about reconciling. We talked about what had gone wrong with our relationship. She was staying at my mother's house. I didn't want to make anybody angry. Rather than officially ending the relationship, I left it up in the air. My future was uncertain. I was involved in a relationship and a case with someone else. There were no guarantees as to how this would work out. Additionally, if I was locked up for an extended period, who was going to stand by me? I didn't want to get locked in on either side.

The next day, Charlotte came to see me. Things were still somewhat distorted between us. We needed to resolve our differences. If we didn't, it would leave room for the detectives to take advantage of the situation. We talked about our relationship and the cases. We were careful not to say anything that would help the detectives. We also talked about my visitor. In the end, I assured her my relationship with Valerie was over. We reconciled our differences. Valerie didn't come back to the jail.

Two months later, we were sentenced. We agreed to a plea bargain. This was the only way to assure Charlotte's freedom. I got a six-year split sentence, four years to serve in prison and two years on probation. Charlotte got probation.

Afterwards, I was sent to a correctional camp in Hardwick, Georgia. It was a state camp, but it had county camp mentality. It was sweet in a lot of ways. It afforded me some opportunities, which reminded me of being free. In the end, it was too sweet. I made some careless mistakes bringing heat on me. It also brought heat on Charlotte.

When I found out she was selling drugs again, I was glad. This gave me an opportunity to contribute to the house and make sure I had plenty of money on the books (my prison account). I became one of her biggest customers. She never brought drugs into the prison. We worked out what we thought was a better system. Hopefully, this glitch in the system has been fixed. The officers searched my room and locker looking for drugs. This was to no avail. An officer warned me beforehand, they were coming. He came with them for the search. His warning gave me an opportunity to get straight. With Charlotte coming to visit me every week, I had been able to send most of my money home.

After they searched me, I wasn't overly concerned about Charlotte. I knew she wouldn't come into the prison dirty. They searched me on a Friday night. The procedure for making a telephone call was complicated. There wasn't time for me to warn her. She was coming the next day. Another inmate informed me his wife had been searched during an earlier visitation period. I was sure they were going to search Charlotte. From my window, I saw her drive up. Discreetly, I tried to warn her. When she entered the prison, she was searched. Knowing how she felt about taking off her clothes, I was disgusted. There was nothing I could do about it. After nothing was found on her, they allowed us to visit. I tried to console and reassure her. Rivers would never be the same for us.

In a week, I was moved to another prison. This was better for both of us. I was closer to home. She wouldn't have to make the long drives to see me. My time at Rutledge went smoothly. Charlotte was still working the drug business. We put a hold on my end of it. I enrolled in a program to enable me to become a licensed barber. Despite this, I planned to return to crime when I was released.

It was getting close to my release date. Charlotte was afraid. She was concerned about a voice she was hearing. The voice warned her she was going to get caught selling the drugs. She was ready to quit. I knew God was real, but I was hoping this was paranoia. The business was going too good. It was something I could build upon when I was released. If she could hold on for another month, I could take over the business.

God's Grace

*Behold now, Thy servant hath found grace in Thy sight,
and Thou hast magnified Thy mercy, which Thou hast
shewed unto me in saving my life; and I cannot escape to
the mountain, lest some evil take me, and I die:*
Genesis 19:19

Four of us were arrested that day. During this time, 'Something' was still watching over me. When we arrived at the jail, everybody was strip searched, with the exception of me. The cocaine was still on me and I was scared the detectives would find it. If they had told me they were going to search me, I probably would have passed out from fear. We were taken to the holding cells. The men were housed in a separate part of the jail. I was given clothes to change into. This had been delayed as long as possible. I had assured the officers my bondsman would pick me up immediately. He didn't show up. Subsequently, Denna and I were taken to the third floor. We were placed in the same cell.

I had successfully gotten the drugs into the jail. However, I wasn't going to be caught with them or risk getting caught taking them back out. I didn't want to waste money by flushing the drugs. Only a few of the inmates in the cell would merit being included in the party that took place. Comet and baby powder was sprinkled everywhere to kill the smell of the burning drugs. A couple of people smoked the cocaine in cigarettes. In exchange for a pack of Bugle tobacco, I gave another inmate a rock of cocaine.

It seemed a small price to pay considering the circumstances. Bugle reminded me of marijuana. This was the way I smoked the cocaine.

With the cocaine gone, I needed a plan to get us out of this mess. Getting out on bond had never been a problem for me before, but this time my bondsman was taking his time. I wasn't worried. Somebody was going to get me out. It just needed to be quick. A bigger problem worried me. Denna and I were both on probation. My probation officer had warned me if I was ever arrested for drugs, he would recommend violating my probation. Sitting in the cell, I began to prepare one plan for Denna and one for me. After a few days, I was released on bond. I was able to secure Denna's release the next day.

After my release, I wanted my mother's help. I needed her help. I wanted prayer and lots of it. A miracle was what I needed. It wasn't justice I needed. If there was anything I understood, it was where miracles come from. My fear led me to repent. I also began to cry out to God in away I hadn't in years. He was the one to help me. He had been trying for months to help me, but to no avail. After my arrest, I wanted His help desperately.

Before Buck was released, I received the Baptism of the Holy Ghost and joined a prayer band. All of the scriptures I had ever learned came back to my memory. I was able to rightly divide the 'Word of Truth.' I gave up smoking marijuana and drinking champagne. I also stopped hanging out with Denna. This didn't go over well with her. All my time was spent reading the Word, in prayer meetings, Bible study, and going to church.

As a result of the arrest, I was placed on intensive probation. Additionally, I was given community service hours to complete. These requirements were a small price to pay for my freedom. I was also given a new probation officer. Mr. Green was very nice and went to bat for me, trying to ensure I remained free. It appeared I was complying with the new terms. Believing the intensive probation and community service were sufficient punishment for the crime, he began conferring with the judge, requesting this serve as my sentence. After a couple of months, he was going to place me back on regular probation, but decided he needed to wait until a final decision was made in my case. His negotiations with the judge weren't going the way he expected. He didn't want anyone to think he had been too easy on me.

Be ye not unequally yoked together with unbelievers: for what fellowship hath righteousness with unrighteousness? and what communion hath light with darkness?
2 Corinthians 6:14

Trying to reconcile my salvation with my living arrangements, I began witnessing to Buck. He promised me that when he came home things would be different and he would give up the drugs. He was due to come home within weeks. My divorce had been final for several months. I knew we wouldn't be able to continue living together without us being married, if I was to maintain my salvation. I knew the scripture about being unequally yoked with unbelievers. Desperation began to work with me. Once he was released, he didn't follow through on any of his promises. He immediately began the same habits leading to his previous arrests. The first day he was out, he got high off heroin. Within the week, he was stealing again. Desperate to correct the problem, I began to use The Word to condemn his behavior.

Something else happened when Buck first came home. This increased my pleadings. The day after he was released we went to the parole office. There was a requirement that upon your release from prison on parole in the state of Georgia you report to your parole officer, within twenty-four-hours. Buck informed the parole officer we lived together before he was locked up and we were planning to be married. The officer agreed he could move back into the house with me. That was until he read Buck's record and realized who his co-defendant was. Buck had to return to the parole office the next day. Again, I was with him. When we entered his office together, he responded angrily.

"I should have locked you up yesterday when you came in here with her."

He would be making home visits to assure Buck was at his mother's house each night before midnight. This began a struggle for us to juggle both a 10:00 p.m. and a midnight curfew. The problem was that sometimes my probation officers didn't come until almost midnight. Some nights, it would be so late that we mistakenly assumed they weren't coming.

There was a ten-minute ride between locations. Most of the time, we were able to make the transition without a hitch. However, there were a couple of narrow escapes. If my probation officers arrived late and his parole officer arrived early, we had a problem. One of Buck's sisters lived in the house next to his mother. A row of bushes and trees separated their driveways. On more than one occasion, they served as a shield to the back door of the house. If the officer was knocking at the front door, I waited in the car until he completed his visit. However, most of the time, I was waiting in an adjacent room.

God's Grace: The Flip Side

Now therefore, I pray thee, if I have found grace in Thy sight, shew me now Thy way, that I may know Thee, that I may find grace in Thy sight: and consider that this nation is Thy people. Exodus 33:13

It was less than a month before my release. When Charlotte came to see me, she told me she had been arrested. I was shocked. This was not the way I had planned for things to happen. We were so close to making the drug business work. She also told me she had given her life back to God. I was glad about this. However, this began a new cycle in our life.

So she cried whenever she was with him and kept it up for the rest of the celebration. At last, on the seventh day, he told her the answer because of her persistent nagging. Judges 14:17a

I knew a lot of things about her. During this period, I found out something new, she was a nag. She wanted us to get married. She wanted me stop doing drugs. Most of all, she wanted me to be "saved". She harped on this every time she came to see me. I promised her I would do right by her when I was released. At the time, I wanted to believe what I was telling her. It was never my intention to deceive her. Outwardly, I needed to appear strong for her. She needed my support. I could handle prison. This wasn't something I wanted for her. Prison was no joke. Inside, I was hurting. Everything was going wrong. I couldn't believe what was happening. The desire to medicate was still there. As my release date grew closer, the desire to medicate increased. It became stronger and more urgent.

It is better to dwell in a corner of the housetop, than with a brawling woman in a wide house. Proverbs 21:9

The day I was released, Charlotte picked me up from the prison. I wanted to stop by Herb's house. She was uncomfortable with this stop. I kept my true intentions hidden from her. As she was sitting on the porch with Herb's wife, I took my medication in the bathroom. It didn't take long for her to figure it out. This was when the nagging escalated. Once the nagging started, I didn't think it would ever end.

The next day, I reported to the parole office. My parole officer told me we wouldn't be able to live together. I asked him why.

"She's your co-defendant."

I assured him that was in the past. I told him she had changed. He thought this was an excuse. He also called me John Henry. He talked to me like I was nothing. He was the worst officer I ever met. In the end, I disregarded everything he said. He did everything he could to provoke me to anger. No matter what he said, I remained calm. In this situation, he had the upper hand. He had the ability to manipulate my freedom.

When we left his office, we needed to come up with a plan. Stealing was my game. As a result of his stipulations, I needed to steal time with her. With the threat of her going to prison, I wanted to spend as much time as possible with her. We found a way to make it work. It took a lot of juggling, but we never spent one night apart. He tried to catch us, but he never accomplished his mission.

She didn't go stealing with me anymore. Most of the time, she dropped me off in Wynnton. She gave me a lunch to take with me. Normally, I told her what time to pick me up. There were other times when she just popped up. If I stayed gone too long, I knew she would come looking for me. She was good at finding me. If I wasn't ready to go in, I left messages for her to wait for me. She waited and she nagged.

Sometimes, she nagged herself to sleep. If she woke up and I was still awake, she nagged some more. She nagged me about eating. She nagged me about sleeping. She nagged me about stealing. She was afraid I would overdose. She nagged me about going to church. In between the nagging, she prayed. When she finished praying, she quoted scriptures, but she never forgot to nag. It was part of the cycle.

Pray Without Ceasing

And shall not God avenge His own elect, which cry day and night unto Him, though He bear long with them?
Luke 18:7

Immediately, God had my undivided attention. He was no longer 'Something.' He was 'God.' This time, I was really scared I might have to go to prison. The thought of going to prison wasn't appealing to me. Actually, I found the thought repulsive. My mother was very patient with me, regardless of my consistent failures. She never washed my face in my mistakes. This wasn't the time for me to be hanging out in the streets and I had no desire to be in the streets. Everybody was praying for me. People came to my house to pray for me and I went to other houses for prayer. They weren't just praying. They were expecting answers to the prayers. God was answering the prayers. There was one problem, the answer. Repeatedly the answer came back, "When you go to court, tell the truth." This wasn't exactly what I wanted to hear them say.

Likewise the Spirit also helpeth our infirmities: for we know not what we should pray for as we ought: but the Spirit itself maketh intercession for us with groanings that cannot be uttered. And He that searcheth the hearts knoweth what is the mind of the Spirit, because He maketh intercession for the saints according to the will of God. And we know that all things

work together for good to them that love
God, to them who are the called according
to His purpose. Romans 8:26-28

Continuously, I searched for a Word from the Lord on my situation. The answers I was getting weren't specific enough to ease my troubled and worried mind. It didn't make sense to me I should tell the truth. The truth was I was guilty. What I wanted was a miracle. I didn't want justice; I wanted mercy. I wanted to be told I wouldn't have to go prison. Trying to rationalize what I was being told, I informed my lawyer no matter what happened, I wouldn't be able to testify. This wasn't consistent with what I had been told, but this was as close as my fear would let me come to the truth. In my mind, as long as I didn't lie, I was telling the truth. There was no understanding God was giving me instructions to voluntarily tell what had happened in the house that day.

Desperation was setting in on me. I needed answers. I needed Buck to be "saved". In the car there were scriptures taped everywhere. There were also signs, which said no smoking, or profanity was allowed in the car. Also, I searched the car every time he came home. I gave him enough Word to choke him. For this, God convicted me, immediately.

One Sunday, after being particularly hard on Buck, God revealed to me the transgression of my ways. Buck had promised me if I went to bed, without continuously worrying him he would go to church with me the next day. He wanted to be left alone to finish getting high, without me 'blowing' (ruining) the high. I left him alone. The next morning, he didn't follow through on his promise. Angrily, I began quoting scriptures to him. He gave no indication he heard one word; therefore, I gave him additional scriptures. He never gave any response. This began a new cycle in our relationship. It went something like this: nagging, ignoring, anger, frustration, eviction, conviction, repentance, honeymoon, kicking the habit, drug abuse, nagging, and the cycle continued.

I drove to church, without Buck. As I was driving, I tried to get my thoughts under control. We were taking communion that Sunday at church. The pastor instructed us to search ourselves to see if we were worthy to partake of the supper. As I sat there asking God to search my heart, a voice whispered to me.

"You're not worthy. What you just did caused a deep hurt."

Buck had shown no signs he ever heard a word said to him. God gently reminded me it is with kindness and love that He draws men to Him. My intentions were good; my words were taken directly from the Word of God. The scriptures hadn't been taken out of context. Nonetheless, I had carefully chosen each scripture to force Buck to see his wretchedness. Each time, he didn't respond to my words, a firmer scripture pronouncing judgment was quoted. My words had been sharp and they had pierced Buck to the bone.

> Do not lie in wait like an outlaw at the home
> of the godly. And don't raid the house
> where the godly live. They may trip seven
> times, but each time they will rise again.
> But one calamity is enough to lay the
> wicked low. Proverbs 24:15-16

As the time for my case to be brought to court drew closer, it became increasingly obvious there would be no plea bargain. Weighing heavily on my mind was, "Tell the truth." Again, I reminded my attorney I wouldn't be able to testify. However, I never explained my rationale for this statement.

As the trial progressed, each witness lied to suit his or her own purposes. Pete had cut a deal in exchange for the charges being dropped against him. It sounded like he was an unwilling victim, who was forced to use drugs. He told his jaded view of everything on the witness stand. This included the process of injecting drugs intravenously. He said had received the drugs from me. He conveniently forgot he had requested the drugs from me. "Beg" is probably more accurate. There were many times when I thought about getting even with him. However, I didn't have to. We were blessed never to see each other again. He escaped going to prison. He never escaped the lifestyle. Years later, he died a violent death, which was drug related. Ironically, the lawyer who represented him has since been arrested, on drug related charges. It was rumored the lawyer was the biggest drug dealer in the area.

There was another person who was arrested in the house with us. He refused to testify and the charges were dropped against him.

My lawyer told me I would have to testify, since all blame was being placed firmly on me. The thought of taking the stand was horrifying to me and this was extremely obvious. While on the witness stand, I was so nervous I began to pop chewing gum and stutter profusely. In my mind was ringing, "Tell the truth." How could I tell the truth? The judge instructed me to take the chewing gum out of my mouth. I fumbled miserably throughout my testimony.

Although, the detectives had testified the amount of cocaine found on the mirror was too small to measure, the possession of cocaine was the more serious of the two charges. My Aunt Bobbie was in the courtroom with me. She encouraged me to leave town to avoid going to prison. I didn't want to run for the rest of my life. I decided I would tough this out, although, the thought of going to prison was repulsive to me.

And of whom hast thou been afraid or feared, thou hast lied, and hast not remembered Me, nor laid it to thy heart? have not I held My peace even of old, and thou feareth Me not?
Isaiah 57:11

When Buck and I got married, I wanted to be the Proverbs kind of wife. I just never saw this example. Our marriage started crazy from the beginning. We both felt pressured to get married because it was obvious I was going to prison. The state of Georgia has strict rules about ex-felons. We knew it would be a problem for us to continue our relationship with me in prison and him on parole. During the court recess, Buck and I were married.

Resigned I was going to prison, I didn't want to go broke. I needed enough money to last until I was released. By my calculations, under the Georgia Parole Guidelines, I would only serve four to five months. I needed at least five hundred dollars. We went stealing and I got the funds I needed. Afterwards, I got a bottle of champagne and a bag of marijuana. That night, I went to bed, leaving Buck up getting high. The day's events had exhausted me. The next morning, I grabbed another bottle of champagne, a champagne glass, and a couple of joints, and we headed to court for my sentence.

The judge gave me a fifteen-year sentence for the possession of cocaine and ten years for the possession of marijuana. Both sentences would run concurrent. He had given me the maximum sentence for the charge. If only I had "Told the truth." Denna was given ten years for each count of possession. This sentence would also run concurrent.

When we arrived at the jail, I took my Bible to my room and placed it up under my pillow. This position was chosen to keep the Word literally near my head. This gave me the assurance I wouldn't lose my mind under the weight of the sentence. The penal system is not the place to show weakness. Outwardly, I needed to appear strong. Inwardly, I was afraid to entertain the possibility of being gone more than a few months. I never gave way to the thought of serving more than a few months.

Jailhouse lawyers (inmates) began to define my future. According to their calculations, I would spend at least five to seven years in prison before being released on parole. My confession was unwavering; I would be locked up for four to five months. I needed to believe this if I was going to keep my sanity. I began to research similar cases. I watched every prison sentence in the newspaper. I began writing letters to every agency that might be able to help me get my sentence reversed.

> *Let not them that are mine enemies wrongfully rejoice over me: neither let them wink with the eye that hate me without a cause.* Psalm 35:19

Pray Without Ceasing: The Flip Side

*I prayed to the LORD and said, `O Sovereign LORD, do
not destroy Your own people.* Deuteronomy 9:26

It was growing closer to her court date. There was
still no plea bargain. It was weighing heavily on my mind. I
didn't tell her. It was easier to keep my thoughts to myself.
Medicating helped me pretend it wasn't going to happen.
She wasn't going to prison. We talked constantly, when
we were together. We tried to figure out a way to avoid
her going to prison. I tried to convince her to leave town
with me. She didn't want to spend the rest of her life
running from the charges. Maybe she could get probation.
I was praying she wouldn't get any time. It was a sinner's
prayer, but I was praying. Our future was uncertain. We
needed help.

It would be easier if Denna took the charges. With a
previous drug conviction, things were stacked against her.
It was also her house. From everything that had
happened, it appeared she was the one who had been set
up. Nothing was going to change for her if Charlotte went
to prison. In fact, we could help her from the outside.
That's when I decided to make her an offer. If she would
cut Charlotte loose, I was willing to pay her. She would
also have everything she needed before she went to
court. She needed someone to look out for her.

The day I went to see her, Charlotte was with me.
Hoping to make her feel comfortable, I parked the car out
of view. I didn't want her to see Charlotte. My

conversation with her got nowhere. Rather than listening to me, she talked about how good I looked. There was only one purpose for my trip. I wasn't interested in anything else. She was stuck in one place. If Charlotte wasn't going to jail, she didn't want to go. If she was going, she was taking Charlotte with her.

By the time I got back to the car, I was more confused. Why was she so determined? They were supposed to be friends, even distant cousins. What had happened?

"What did you do to her? Why is she trying so hard to take you down? Did something happen before the bust? Is there something you aren't telling me?"

"I don't have the answers to your questions. Those are questions you should have asked her."

When we left there, we rode through Ninth Street. I saw my buddy, Mike. When I told him about what had happened, he said he would try to talk to her. She stuck with her plan.

Maybe the lawyer would be able to help. We talked to our lawyer a couple of times. There would be no plea bargain for Charlotte, if Denna didn't agree to one. They were going to try to make her an offer she couldn't refuse. They didn't know what she had in mind. She was going to refuse any offer that didn't include Charlotte going to prison.

Charlotte had gone overboard with her vows to God. I had seen people committed to God, but nothing like this. There were memos all over the car. One night, Mike got in the car with me.

"Buck, what is that?"

"Mike, don't start."

I had just encouraged him to continue with his best shot at teasing me. He poured it on. He was teasing me bad. I understood the purpose, but he almost caused me to laugh. I held it back. If I had laughed, he would have really continued joking.

"Man, what's wrong with Charlotte? You can just let me out on the next corner."

I made a gesture to pull over.

"I was just playing man."

There were times she tried to force me into salvation. My mind was far from what she was saying. In the future, I planned to get "saved", but not now. I wanted God to help her. However, I wasn't ready yet. There would be time in the future. She was nagging nonstop. The more she nagged, the more medication I wanted. She had a scripture for everything and she didn't mind sharing them. She nagged my friends and me. I didn't bring any of my friends near the house. They weren't trying to come. It was better to be quiet and let her have it.

During this time, she wouldn't take any money or clothes from me. There were three things she wanted, freedom, my salvation, and to get married. The answers were all looking negative. As the court date drew closer, it looked worse. Finally, I decided if she was going to prison, I was going to marry her before it happened. The salvation part could hold.

The day we had dreaded arrived. There were two sicknesses eating at me. My habit was calling, but I had to be in court. My medication had to be worked around court. The thought of losing my woman was also making me sick. It was the craziest thing I had ever seen. There was a brief glimmer of hope. Our attorney told us the prosecution was hopeful. Maybe Denna would accept a new offer. They were going to offer her a year. She had already served several months on a probation revocation, which would count towards the year. Hope didn't last long. She responded as usual.

"How much time would Charlotte serve?"

Aunt Bobbie came down to go to court with her. This was good support. No one else had mentioned going. She took time off from work and came down from Atlanta. As the trial progressed, we were both worried. It appeared we had a common plan. It would be better for Charlotte to skip the rest of the trial and leave town. She was being railroaded. We knew the DA had a witness waiting to testify against her. The lawyer tried his best. It just wasn't enough.

This was a new experience for me. I had never seen anyone openly snitch. Pete described his version of incident. I had never seen such a coward, but there he was in open court. I sat there, amazed, shocked, and growing angry. It would be easy to hurt him for what he did to her. In the end, I didn't have to do anything. It wasn't long before his pettiness caught up with him. Someone else took his life.

We had taken blood tests weeks earlier. I loved her, but I wasn't ready to get married. I put it off until the last minute. The possibility of her conviction was the primary reason for our marriage. If she wasn't convicted, we could delay the marriage. If she was convicted, there would be too many complications if we weren't married. When the court recessed for lunch, we got married. For lunch we had champagne. I also had some medication. At the end of the day, the hearing was continued until the following day. Resolved she was going to prison, she had one statement.

"I'm not going broke."

There was no reason for her to go broke. I knew what to do. For the first time since I had been home, she went stealing with me. It was different this time. We were successful at every store we picked. We were stealing for a different reason. Everything needed to be sold before we went home, except the outfits she had decided to keep. It was morning when we made it in. Charlotte drank champagne and smoked weed all day. She managed to laugh about her situation. It was a different laugh. She was laughing, in spite of the pain.

When she was locked up the next day, I had good intentions. She had stood by me and I planned to stick by her. Finally, the seriousness of the situation sunk in. When I got home, she wouldn't be there to nag me. It didn't take long before the drugs had total control. My mother was concerned about me. She was so concerned she went to the jail and told Charlotte everything I had been doing. She didn't have the entire facts straight, but she gave her enough information to make her suspicious. When I went to see her, she was ready to hit me with the things she had heard. Things were already spinning out of control.

Charlotte warned me about what I was doing. This didn't mean much to me. The odds were against me. If I kept going into the same stores, I was going to be caught. Nevertheless, I kept going to the same spots.

Charlotte Russell

The Honeymoon

*And Jesus answering said unto them, The children of this
world marry, and are given in marriage:* Luke 20:34

We had some kind of honeymoon. It will never be
forgotten. The honeymoon suite wasn't exactly the
executive suite or the penthouse. It was bunk with
whomever you can until you can get a private room, or
more appropriately, find a place to put your mattress on
the floor of one of the cells. There was room service, but
no choices from the menu. The food was passed through
the flap in the wall. There was no private jacuzzi.
However, there was a public shower without doors. It had
windows facing the main hall. Anyone walking by could
observe you bathing. Additionally, anyone sitting in the
day room of the cell could observe the ritual. This was a
point of contention for me because people wanted to see
my scars. There was no way I was going to accommodate
their desire. Rather than endure the humiliation, I took
birdbaths in my room. There was no plush carpet, but a
concrete floor. There was no down filled bed and satin
sheets, but instead I had a metal bed with a thin twin
plastic mattress. There were midnight chats, as the other
inmates discussed how crazy I was to keep saying I would
be going home in a few months.

I spent the first two weeks of the honeymoon
without my husband, communicating regularly through the
mail. Before the end of the month, my new husband joined
me for the honeymoon. However, he was not coming to

share my suite. There was a separate suite reserved for him, with his name on it.

And afterward, I will pour out my Spirit on all people. Your sons and daughters will prophesy, your old men will dream dreams, your young men will see visions.
Joel 2:28 (NIV)

The dreams started while I was locked up in the county jail. Mama had sickened me with her dreams. She was always dreaming something about me. She was always warning me I was going to get caught. The dreams were so real. They were so accurate. I knew the source of her dreams. In spite of these facts, I resented her dreams. Then it started. I started having my own dreams.

Before this time, I never remembered having a dream. The first dream came and it scared me. In the dream, Buck was headed north bound on Interstate 185. As he approached the Macon Road exit, he was approaching a roadblock. It was a trap. They were waiting for him. It didn't take much for me to figure out this dream.

If you are a thief, stop stealing. Begin using your hands for honest work, and then give generously to others in need.
Ephesians 4:28 (NLT)

Near this exit, there was a particular store. It was a thief's paradise. It was also one of his favorite stores. I warned him not to go back into the store. This was before I had the dream. After the dream, I warned him again. He listened to me the same way I had listened to Mama. He ignored my warnings. He never knew when to quit.

He hit this store again and again. Then it happened. I got the word. Buck was downstairs in the holding cell. When his co-defendant made it to the floor, she sent me a message. They had been busted at thief's paradise. The store had finally learned to use the numerous video cameras in the store. Buck had been caught on tape during a previous theft. When they walked into the store, the doors were locked. Guns were also drawn. They were arrested. Nevertheless, it was already too late for the store. By this time, every thief in Wynnton must have known about the store. What possessed them to open the store so close to Wynnton, with the backdoor unlocked? It was packed with electronics, televisions, video recorders, stereo systems, and video cameras. Everyone within five miles of Wynnton should have known to keep the doors locked, especially the back door. This store was in walking distance and there was no security on the back door. The store soon went out of business. It was their stupidity, which led to its closing as much as the thieves who found the store too sweet to resist.

Buck had ignored all of my warnings to stop stealing. Pleading is probably more accurate. I had repeatedly warned him about this specific store. I had begged him not to go back there. This is where he was caught. His arrest wasn't really a surprise to me. Still, his being locked up made me angry with him. I didn't know when I would see him again. In addition, I had stood by him while he was incarcerated; he had a responsibility to do the same for me. Him standing by me was actually more of a fantasy I had. I knew drugs were his first love. Eventually, the drugs would interfere with anything he was planning to do for me. I understood the hold the addiction had on his life.

He was assigned to the fifth floor and I was housed on the third floor. He arranged to secure the room directly above mine. The Muscogee County Jail has a unique communication system. The toilets are connected between the floors. If you pumped the water in the toilet out and disinfected the toilet with Comet, newspaper could be used to make a kind of horn. The horn extended from the toilet allowing your voice to travel through the newspaper and through the pipes. Thus, you were able to talk between floors. This was how we spent our honeymoon, bent over the toilet talking to each other.

Buck was calm about the whole thing, almost relieved the suspense was over. Nevertheless, my mind was torn. The sooner I was sent off to prison, the sooner I would be able to make parole. However, being sent off also meant I wouldn't be able to talk to him or see him. Talking to him helped keep me from dwelling on the length of my sentence. This experience had given us some time to do some limited bonding.

This was a time when our friendship really developed. It was perhaps here that we began to develop our nonverbal communication skills. Hear me out. How can you develop nonverbal communication skills without looking at the person with whom you are communicating? While utilizing the communication system at the jail, it was also possible for other people to hear portions of your conversations. If the toilet was pumped out on other floors in the line, it became a party line (shared line).

The honeymoon lasted for a couple of months before I changed suites and the extended honeymoon began. I was in the next group of women prisoners sent to Hardwick, Georgia. At this time, the only women's prison in the state was located in Hardwick.

Early one morning, the names were called of the people who were leaving in fifteen minutes for the prison in Hardwick. My name was one of about twelve names called. Hurriedly, I tried to wake Buck up so I could say goodbye, while at the same time throwing my limited belongings into a pillowcase. About 6:30 a.m., we were shipped off to Hardwick. My heart was broken. I would miss him, greatly.

When I got to Hardwick, my nagging got worse. Nagging was going to be a routine part of our relationship for many years. I didn't know how to submit. I was comfortable being in charge. While being locked up at the jail, there were a number of things I wanted to ask Buck about. The time hadn't been right. He was sick. The toilet had ears. I didn't want the other inmates to know I was upset with him. None of his explanations added up. There was constant gossip in the cell. Now that I was away from jail, there were a few questions needing answers. Gossip in the prison was going to add more questions. When I confronted him with the gossip, he lied and offered weak explanations. Nevertheless, he was my support system. Consequently, I had to put some of my questions on hold until we were both free.

In the meanwhile, I buried my anger deep within my heart. The pain was hidden on the outside. This was not the place to display my hurt or embarrassment. Inside of me, my resentment was brewing. I was never one to leave a debt unsettled. I paid all my bills. Every effort was made to pay them on time. This one would be late, but it would be paid. I could have chosen to forgive him. This may have been an option if I had been able to deal with the hurt immediately. The circumstances being what they were I would have to deal with the pain upon my release.

Sitting in my small cell, I began to reminiscence. Running through my mind were all the long hours I had spent traveling down the highway to see him. During his incarceration, I never missed an opportunity to visit him. He never missed a store date. There was always money in his account. Each month, I had shipped him a package. In more than one way, I had put my freedom in jeopardy to ensure his comfort while being locked up. To make matters worse, there was the humiliation of being "strip searched". This was my most painful memory. I hated taking my clothes off in front of family. Having to take them off in front of the prison guard was really traumatic for me. There was a lot to be angry about. There was a lot to resent him for. He had shown his gratitude for my efforts. He repaid me with infidelity and lies. Now, I had time on my hands to ponder his actions. What did I mean to him? There was a lot to think about and I the time to indulge in it.

And said, For this cause shall a man leave father and mother, and shall cleave to his wife: and they twain shall be one flesh? Wherefore they are no more twain, but one flesh. What therefore God hath joined together, let not man put asunder.
Matthew 19:5-6

Jim had been trying to get me back. The door had been closed. I didn't want him. I wasn't satisfied with him. I wasn't satisfied with Buck. In fact, I wasn't satisfied with myself. Buck had hurt me immensely. In the past, when I had been hurt, I ran to Jim for comfort. It was part of the cycle. He wasn't there physically inside of the prison, but the door was open again. He was my security blanket. Jim was keeping tabs on Buck. He told me this from the beginning of my relationship with Buck.

"I'm waiting for him to mess up. He will. He doesn't know what he has, I do. I know what it's like to take you for granted. When he does, I'll be there."

His words were never forgotten. Still, I never gave him any indication Buck was messing up. My pride wouldn't let me. He found out from people in the street. Buck was taking me for granted. If anybody understood this, it was Jim. The things Buck did bruised my ego. The things Jim said made me feel special again. Before I had been chasing Jim. Now, he was chasing me. As long as Buck continued his lifestyle, I was going to continue listening to Jim. We were only friends. However, he made me feel desired. He knew I was never coming back to him. He understood he had hurt me for the last time. He was never going to take me for granted again. It was a lesson Buck was yet to learn.

Immediately, upon our arrival at the prison, we were fingerprinted and photographed again. We were provided with wardrobes for our stay consisting of three pairs of khaki-colored pants with matching short sleeve tops. We were assigned rooms in a section of the prison referred to as Diagnostics. These buildings were separated from the main prison population by a locked fence. The inmates who were in isolation or on Death Row were also housed in this area of the prison. Whenever new prisoners arrived, the other prisoners wanted to get a look at them. They were also anxious to get the news from home.

The prison at Hardwick was set up like a college dormitory for women. With the exception of the barbed wire fence surrounding the prison and the guards, there were no indications this was a prison. Prisoners were allowed to wear their own shoes and accessories. Occasionally, you would see an inmate who was in solitary confinement. White jumpsuits and handcuffs on their hands identified them. Sometimes, there were also shackles on their feet serving as further identification. They were prisoners within the prison. At first glance, this appeared to be a co-ed prison. It took me a few minutes to realize some of the men in khaki-colored uniforms were actually women.

We were allowed to spend a maximum of $25 dollars a week at the prison store. Make no mistake about it; we never forgot we were in prison. Each inmate was assigned a counselor. This was the person I wanted to meet. I hoped she would have some answers for me. Within a few days, the meeting took place. When I told her by my calculations, I would only serve four to five months, she stated she didn't know of anybody with my charges having a sentence even close to mine. I assured her I would only be there for only a few months.

The parole board was running slow in sending out parole decisions. When I received my guideline back, the board had deviated from the grid recommendations of four to five months and added six months to the time I was required to serve in prison. By this time, I had already served six months. I would be going home in four to five months.

Buck had been assigned to Jack T. Rutledge State Prison in Columbus. We had received special permission to write each other and were communicating regularly. The band from Jack Rutledge was coming to perform at the women's prison in Hardwick. We learned we might be able to obtain special permission for Buck to travel with the band for a special visit with me. This would require approval from the warden at both prisons. This worked out and we were able to have a visit lasting several hours. This was the highlight of my prison stay. Of course, the visit was monitored closely.

Look thou upon me, and be merciful unto me, as Thou usest to do unto those that love Thy name. Order my steps in Thy word: and let not iniquity have dominion over me. Deliver me from the oppression of man: so that I will keep Thy precepts. Make Thy face to shine upon Thy servant; and teach me Thy statutes. Psalm 119:132-135

After being incarcerated for eleven months, I was finally released. My friend, Esther drove down to pick me up. My mother and children came with her. When we got back to Columbus, they dropped me off at Jack Rutledge to see Buck. This was a surprise visit for him. He knew it was getting close to my release date. However, I hadn't notified him of the actual date. This would begin my weekly visits to the prison to see him. I had survived my own prison ordeal.

Lord how they are increased that trouble me! Many are they that rise up against me. Many are they that wish to say of my soul, There is no help for him in God. But thou, O Lord, art a shield for me; my glory, and the lifter up of mine head. I cried unto the Lord with my voice, and He heard me out of His holy hill. I laid me down to sleep; I awakened for the Lord sustained me. I will not be afraid of ten thousands people, that have set themselves against me round about. Psalm 3:1-6

My intention upon my release was to get actively involved in a good church. I went to church a couple of times after I got out, but not consistently. Procrastination and complacency made it easy for me to lose sight of my promises to God. It seemed the only thing I had really made up my mind about was I didn't want to sell drugs again. My prison sentence, if I was caught, was already defined: fourteen years and one month. This sentence was long enough to make any sane person think twice about committing another crime.

Henry L. Johnson

The Honeymoon: The Flip Side

Marriage is honourable in all, and the bed undefiled: but whoremongers and adulterers God will judge.
Hebrews 13:4

There was an electronics store that was sweet. They were giving their merchandise away. It was hard to resist the temptation to keep hitting them. The store hadn't been open long. They made the mistake of moving too close to Wynnton. It didn't take long for their weakness to be discovered. When I went into the store the last time, it was a trap. They had us on videotape from a previous theft. They had already discovered our identities. A warrant had been issued for our arrest. They were waiting on us. When we walked into the store, they locked the door. The police were there, instantly.

Actually, I had gone so far with the drugs I was ready for a break. This would give me a chance to pull myself together. I needed the vacation. Honestly, jail is a good place to get a break. I was already hurting about the fifteen years CJ had been given. Since we were married, I called Charlotte "CJ." The drugs had hindered me from doing what I needed to do for her. I needed to talk to her, but I wasn't looking forward to it. She needed me to be on the outside. I was already behind in writing to her. At least one visitation period had been missed.

Whenever you come into the jail, it seems people are glad to see you. They know you have news from the street. They are eager to hear it. After changing into jailhouse garb, I was taken to the fifth floor. When I got there, the cell was crowded. I had to sleep on a mattress placed on the floor. There were no empty rooms in the cellblock. One of my homeboys let me use his telephone, his toilet. I needed to call CJ. His toilet was already pumped out. He had a friend on the third floor. He asked her to get CJ on the horn.

It was hard to come up with the right words. We needed an honest conversation, but it was a party line. Anyone on several floors with a connecting line pumped out could overhear the conversation. It wasn't as bad as I expected. She made it easy for me to talk to her. It was as if she understood what I was feeling. After I was able to secure my own room, we were able to talk more freely.

By this time, I had gone through the withdrawals. My health was starting to improve. I found the time to workout and regain my strength. My diet consisted of eating as many cat-heads (hard jailhouse biscuits) as I could get my hands on. They would help me to gain weight quickly. Since I didn't smoke, I could use my funds to buy the cat-heads or an extra tray from one of the inmates. Chocolate candy also helped.

During my first months, I spent most of my time on the horn talking to CJ. It eliminated a lot of my worries and made it easier for me to kick the drugs. It was almost like a vacation, considering the circumstances. She was always as close as the horn. In my heart, I knew I needed to be on the outside. This kept haunting me. I explained to her how I felt. She seemed to understand and accepted my explanations. There were lots of things needing to be explained. The party line wouldn't permit this. There were too many listening ears.

After a couple of months, I received a call from her. She awakened me from my sleep. We knew this day was coming. We had expected it for weeks.

"Buck, I'm getting ready to go."

"Okay! Take care baby. I love you. Write me as soon as you get your number."

"Okay! I'll write. I'm gone."

She would need this number before I could write her at the prison. I made my way to a small window in the cell. Maybe, I would be able to see her when she boarded the van or when she walked outside of the jail. After about an hour, I knew she was gone. I hadn't seen her leave. When I went back to my room, I flushed the toilet. That afternoon, I had a friend to check on their departure. It was good for her to get the bid on the way. Still, I felt uneasy. I was going to miss her. It was as if she left twice on the same sentence. Shortly thereafter, we got news the ladies had been transferred. I started counting the days it would take for me to hear from her. In my estimation, it should take two to three days before I got a letter from her.

A nagging wife is as annoying as the constant dripping on a rainy day.
Proverbs 27:15

The letter arrived on time. When I got the letter, it wasn't what I was expecting. She was tripping badly. It was full of accusations. She had heard a lot of negative reports about me. In the letter, she didn't hold back. Other letters followed behind this one. She was mailing letters faster than I could answer them. It was as if I didn't stand a chance. I felt like a victim. Before I could answer one letter, another one arrived. She was hearing rumors about things that had happened during my last bid. There were also reports of what I had been doing on the streets prior to this incarceration. Some of what she was hearing was true. Most of it was exaggerated. I decided to be truthful. I didn't want her to be embarrassed by things I had done while I was in Hardwick.

On my previous sentence, I had been imprisoned at Rivers Correctional Institution. It was near the women's facility. I was enrolled in dental technician classes. These classes were held at the women's prison. That provided temptation. I had wondered how things worked at the women's prison. When I was accepted into the program, it gave me a chance to see first hand. At that time, I had no idea CJ would one day be locked down at this same prison. Many of the women who were housed there on my previous sentence had been released. There was one problem; most of them were back.

This was CJ's first bid. She wasn't giving any indication she was worried about the length of the sentence. They were trying to break her. They wanted her to worry. All of this was done at my expense. I was already worried about her being locked down. To add to this, I had to worry about the garbage she was being fed. They were exaggerating and filling in any details they were uncertain about. This kept me busy writing letters trying to address the attacks on our relationship. This increased my desire for her to be released soon. Her release date couldn't come soon enough.

When my court date came, I was given ten years. Four of these years were to be served on probation. I would be eligible for parole on the remaining six. The probation time would follow the parole time. That's providing I was paroled. After completing diagnostics in Jackson, Georgia, I was assigned to Jack T. Rutledge State Institution.

It was here I learned family members who were incarcerated were allowed special visits under certain circumstances. I went to the library. There I was able to check the state policy. This verified I should be able to visit my wife. While working in the Identification Room, I had learned the prison band was scheduled to perform at the women's prison. I put in a request to travel with them. This would give me a chance to correct things with CJ. My request was approved.

For the first part of the visit, we were allowed to sit in the prison store. It was good to be able to clear the air. At the beginning of the visit, we were allowed one kiss. As the visit ended, we were allowed another kiss. This didn't deter us. The front of the store was enclosed in glass. When the other inmates started arriving for the concert, they were fascinated to see us. The people from Columbus were trying to speak to me. We were asked to move to the auditorium for the concert. We sat at the back of the room. An officer stood nearby. This was an important time for our relationship. I knew the letters would be different.

Shortly after the visit, CJ wrote me to tell me she had made parole. She had been given a month, but not a date. She was scheduled to be released in August. I was glad and relieved. She would be able to visit me.

On a Saturday morning, I received a call to visitation. I expected to see one of my relatives. When I walked in, I looked around for my visitor. She was hiding. My memory of her standing there still sticks out in my mind. It still makes me smile. She was wearing a yellow and white dress. Her hair had been cut in some fancy style. It was full on top and feathered back on the sides. There was a smirk on her face. I was glad to see her. I knew she felt the same way.

I responded, "Look a there! Um huh!"

We embraced. It was good to hold her. It felt like *Love American Style*. She had been released earlier that morning. CJ had been dropped off at the prison. My sister was going to pick her up after our visit. This was the first of many visits. CJ had survived the incarceration. She was back at home with the kids. As soon as I was released, we could move on with our lives.

Blessed is he whose transgressions are forgiven, whose sins are covered.
Psalm 32:1 (NIV)

I thought she had forgiven me for everything happening while she was locked up. It wasn't long before I discovered I was mistaken. She had a vendetta against me. She was planning to make me pay for hurting her.

To keep me from becoming conceited because of these surpassingly great revelations, there was given me a thorn in my flesh, a messenger of Satan, to torment me.
2 Corinthians 12:7

Jim had always wanted her back. He resented the way things had happened. Whenever I was incarcerated, he looked her up. Whenever he called her, she would tell me. I felt as if it was an ego thing for him.

It was as if he was saying, "She was mine all the time."

It was her choice. She could choose whomever she wanted. She chose me. I couldn't understand why she was being fickle. She said she had forgiven me. We survived this, too.

The next year, I completed my incarceration. I was released on parole. We moved on to another phase in our life. The crazy honeymoon was over.

Tally-Ho

Let favor be shewed to the wicked, yet he will not learn
righteousness: in the land of uprightness will he deal
unjustly, and will not behold the majesty of the Lord.
Isaiah 26:10

Now my feet were back on the ground, it would only take me a few days to get another car. This was a necessity for me to function comfortably. I had a grand total of $300 to get the car. My uncle and one of our friends would take me riding to look for the car. We found something, which would suit my needs temporarily. This was all I wanted. I needed something to hold me until I got on my feet. It would be necessary to put oil in the car every day, but at least I was riding. If I had transportation, I could maneuver anything else. I could concentrate on moving out on my own. Before the month was out, I had rented a trailer and moved out.

My mother and I had talked for several years about opening a restaurant. We opened the Tally-Ho Grill without even a dollar to go in the cash register. The menu consisted of a large variety of soul food: chitterlings, ribs, pig feet, pig ears, black-eyed peas, collard greens, macaroni and cheese, and homemade sweet potato pies, etc. We served breakfast, lunch, and dinner. My mother would assist me with the cooking before she went to work each morning. On her lunch hour and again when she finished her regular job with the Housing Authority, she would return to help me with cooking and serving the food.

Buck was excited about the restaurant. However, this excitement wouldn't be prolonged. He was getting close to being released from prison. I had kept my promise not to sell drugs again. I didn't want to go back down that road. Things were going well with my parole. The day he was released, my semi-normal life would be upset again. The first day he was out, I overheard someone offer him a package of crack.

I answered for him, "No, he's not going back to that mess."

There was no way we were going to get involved with this lifestyle again, or so I thought. A few days later, when we returned home from the Tally-Ho, I turned around to tell him something, but he was gone. There were no signs of Buck on the outside of the trailer. My heart fell prostrate. I knew where he had gone.

Determined to teach him a lesson, I drove the car around the street and hid it. I didn't want my friend, Pat to worry if he told her I was missing. Therefore, I went across the street and told her I would be inside the trailer. Since I had bought the trailer while Buck was in prison, he didn't know where the light switches were. The kids were at Mama's house. After turning out all the lights in the house, I laid in Herman's bed and covered up to wait for him. Anxiously, I waited for his return. When he returned, he began fumbling through the house looking for the light switches, to no avail.

He began calling out, "CJ, where are you?"

I laid still and remained silent. Frantically, he went back out the door. I knew he was headed to Pat's trailer. Still, I didn't move. Within a few minutes, the door of the trailer opened again. This time when he returned, he was still screaming, but he was also feeling his way through every room in the house and every inch of the rooms.

Finally, he located my left foot. From there, he found my face, but he was still scared.

"CJ say something! Are you all right?"

Rudely, I responded, "Take your hands off me!"

He didn't tell me he had picked up the package of crack. I don't know how long he thought he would be able to maintain this secret. Sundays were the only days the Tally-Ho was closed. This was our day to go out to an upscale restaurant for dinner. This Sunday, he made a stop and left me in the car, as he went into a relative's house. This was unusual considering where he had stopped. Normally, he would have asked me to come with him.

When he returned, his face confirmed my worst fears. While he had been locked up, many people we knew had begun smoking crack. He didn't know who they were, but I knew quite a few of them. This person was one of them. My decision was to put things on the table. He had given this person a package to sell. They had smoked it up. Knowing he had made grave mistakes in issuing out the packages, I asked him for the names of everyone else who he had given a package to. He gave me one other name.

"Go by to check on your money. Everything you have issued out has gone up in smoke."

His next stop proved me right. This was another person who was hooked on crack. In spite of these mistakes, my desire was not to become involved with moving the drugs. When asked about the quantity of drugs he had picked up, he responded.

"A half a keyload."

A half a keyload is approximately sixteen to eighteen ounces. The actual weight depends on the seller. Wanting to be sure the drugs weren't stashed near my

148

children or me, I asked where they were. This was the most shocking and hurting revelation. An elderly relative was holding the drugs for him. This was more courage than I had and I wasn't actually running short on fortitude.

People started coming by the Tally-Ho prepared to purchase drugs. No matter what was said, they wouldn't believe drugs weren't on the menu. The money started coming fast. I decided it would be necessary for me to get involved, managing the money. My concern was the money would come up short and I would be held accountable for it, too. Things started to get out of hand. Buck was ignoring all my warnings. He brushed my advice off. He thought I was trying to control him. I had learned a hard lesson about helping friends keep their drug business open. He was about to walk over into the same trap.

The more money Buck made selling drugs, the less he desired to work at the Tally-Ho. To compensate for this, he began paying all the expenses of the Tally-Ho. He was constantly buying me things. Every Sunday, he took me to an upscale restaurant. When we left the restaurant, he took me shopping for anything my heart desired. Rather than working, he would give Earline anything she wanted to work in his place. Still, this didn't appease me and my complaining continued.

Earline was in the seventh grade, at this time. Typical of most seventh graders, she became bored with working at the Tally-Ho after school. She wanted to spend more time playing with her friends and participating on the cheerleading squad.

Buck walked into the Tally-Ho one day with some of his old "get high buddies." He told me he was only with them because they were bringing me clothes. Staring him dead in his face, it was obvious his lips were twisted and his mouth was parched. I fell to the floor weeping.

Trying to reassure me, he said, "It was only one time."

His reassurance didn't work. We had been down this road before. We both knew all the intersections and the final destination.

One day, Buck left the Tally-Ho and he was gone for an extremely long time. He didn't call me and this was peculiar. People were continuously coming by the Tally-Ho looking for him, but he was nowhere to be found. It was getting close to the time for the Tally-Ho to close and he still wasn't back. Finally, I called his niece and asked her to pick me up from work. Buck had some crack stashed outside the Tally-Ho. When she picked me up, the crack was taken with me. As we rode down the street, I threw the crack out the window. Later that night, she went back to the spot where I had thrown the drugs. I didn't care. She was welcome to the drugs. I was mad. Drugs were destroying my life.

Our time at home was supposed to be time when we left the stress of the streets behind. Few people had our home telephone number and we didn't sell or keep drugs in the house. One night after we returned home, Buck's niece called and wanted a package. He told her he was in for the night. Knowing she wouldn't take no for an answer, we turned all the lights out in the trailer. I asked Buck if he had hid the crack he had brought home.

He responded by saying, "It's only crumbs. I don't feel like moving it. If she finds it, let her have it."

She had a car you could hear a block away. As we were sitting quietly in the living room, we heard the sound of the ragged car coming. We eased to the kitchen window and watched when she stopped directly in front of the trailer. She didn't come to the door, but instead searched around the back door, going almost immediately to the bag of cookie crumbs (small pieces of crack). We laughed when she got back in the car and drove off.

As the month progressed, another crisis occurred. Buck had been out of drugs for a couple of weeks. David, a friend (what he thought was a friend) of Buck's had asked him to serve as the middleman to pick up cookies (one cookie is an ounce of crack) for him. Jay, the person selling the drugs, wouldn't deal directly with David. Jay knew David, but he didn't trust him. After this exchange had gone a couple of times, Jay asked Buck if he wanted to hold a cookie until the next time David called.

When we arrived home one night, David called. This ticked me off because he wasn't supposed to have our home telephone number. He was asking Buck a lot of questions over the telephone. He asked him if the cookie was whole or cut up. In the background, my protests kept cutting the conversation off. To no avail, I tried to get Buck not to meet him.

Shortly after Buck left the house to meet him, David called back to our home. Originally, Buck was supposed to meet him at his grocery store, David's Grocery. He wanted to change the meeting to a parking lot near a local nightclub. He was trying to get me involved in the transaction. He was rudely instructed to leave me out of that mess. Buck called me after he was unable to locate David. Reluctantly, I gave him the message. Within minutes of him hanging up the telephone, my mother-in-law called to tell me the police were shooting at Buck in her back yard.

Obviously upset, she said, "You need to get here quick. The police are shooting at your husband out here."

Upon my arrival at her house, I pulled up behind David's truck, parked on the left-hand side of the street. Shocked to see David's truck, I forgot momentarily to look for Buck. I was dumb struck to see David wasn't driving the truck. A man with handcuffs extending from the back left pocket of his pants was climbing into the driver's seat of the truck. The complete picture wasn't fully developed, but clearly, the man driving the truck was a detective. The tag number was recorded for future reference. On the right-hand side of the street was parked my brown Cavalier. Buck was nowhere in obvious sight. The front door of the car was open and a detective was getting into the front seat. I walked over to him.

"Excuse me! This is my car."

He responded sure of himself, "This car is being confiscated by the City of Columbus and the police department."

Just as sure, I responded, "Did you find drugs in MY CAR?"

I was sure Buck wouldn't have left the drugs in the car.

He shot back, "No! But the driver of this car has been arrested and he was involved in a drug transaction."

Again, I wanted to know about the drugs, "Did you find any drugs?"

He answered without thinking; "We found a half an ounce of crack in the woods."

Looking around, I didn't see Buck. "Can you tell me what happened to the driver?"

Vaguely, he responded, "You can call the jail later."

Buck had been taken to the hospital, but this wouldn't be known until hours after his arrest. After the police left, I asked Buck's brother to drive me past David's house. His cream colored Toyota truck was parked in his yard. Again, the tag number was verified.

When I got back home, David called me, attempting to offer a pathetic explanation.

"Charlotte, where is Buck?"

Angrily I responded, "You tell me?"

At this point, he started with a lie that didn't even make sense to him.

"I tried to call back to tell him not to meet me. The police kidnapped me and left me handcuffed in the woods. The detectives took my truck. When they came back, I didn't know what they did with it."

Silently, I listened to his explanation. However, I knew what he had done to my husband. Buck called after he was released from the hospital and taken to jail. He told me the police had pistol-whipped him. He wanted me to get him out of jail before his parole officer found out what had happened. This would need to be done quickly.

When Buck was released from jail, there were stitches in the center of his head and bruises covered most of his body. He told me how two officers held him pinned to the ground in the woods, while two others beat him. He further told me that during his time in the holding cell at the jail, he talked to a man who had been busted earlier in the evening. The man said he had been busted with David, but he didn't know what happened to David. I did.

David owed Buck some money. Buck wanted me to pick the money up from him. However, he was afraid my conduct wouldn't be rational. Reluctantly, the call was placed to David and he was informed the money was needed to get Buck out of jail. My uncle went with me to pick the money up from David's house. David was nervous and still trying to explain. With my eyes, I was trying burn a hole in him, so the truth could run out of the hole.

Buck gave me the man's name (Benny Thomas) had been in the holding cell with him. The name is fictitious. I called the jail to find out when the man was scheduled to appear in Recorders Court. Without explaining what had happened to Buck, I asked a lady worked for me at the Tally-Ho to go to this man's hearing along with my daughter. My request was for them to sit at the front of the courtroom. They were to be sure they got all the details of the hearing.

When they returned from court, they had the complete details, not only of this man's arrest, but of Buck's arrest as well. They described everything, including the two telephone calls from the police station were placed to my home. The detectives discussed in open court details of the deal they made with David.

This is how Buck was busted. Benny met a man at a club on Steam Mill Road. The man, who was an undercover detective, asked him if he knew where he could get some crack. The detective promised Benny a small piece of the $20 rock. Benny called David, who lived nearby. This setup led to Benny's and David's arrests.

The detectives offered both of them a deal in exchange for their freedom. If they could give them someone with a larger quantity of drugs, the charges against them would be dropped. When they arrived at the jail, David accepted the deal. He called Buck from the jail to arrange for the setup. Originally, they planned for the arrest to take place at David's store in East Wynnton. When the detectives got to the street where the store was located, too many people were walking around. This was too dangerous to set up the operation. They asked David to call back to our house and change the location of the rendezvous.

When Buck arrived at the store, he didn't see David. He stopped at a telephone booth and called me. He was informed of the second telephone call from David. The second location was in a shopping center on Buena Vista Road, near Buck's mother's house. When Buck pulled up next to David's truck, the detectives jumped out of the truck. A detective grabbed the locked car door, as Buck sped off heading for familiar woods, behind his mother's house. They were right behind him. Buck managed to throw the drugs into the woods before the detectives ran him down. Somehow, the ounce of crack was a half an ounce of crack when it reached the jail.

To avoid going back to jail, Buck left town for a while. His old parole officer began looking for him. This included watching the Tally-Ho and dropping in frequently. This probably helped to ruin business at the Tally-Ho. Many of the customers had illegal occupations or connections. Some of my best customers were drug dealers. Some of them tried their own products. Eventually, they were consuming most of their products. At this point, it became difficult for them to purchase a slice of pie. Crack ruined business at the Tally-Ho in more than one way. The restaurant had been opened more than a year. The Tally-Ho was more work than we had imagined. I had also gotten accustomed to having quick and fast money again.

The finance company was able to get my car back from the police department, after a couple of months. When a drunk driver ran into the car it was decided, it was time to close the Tally-Ho. I wasn't seriously hurt, but this gave me the excuse I needed to close the restaurant.

Tally-Ho: Flip Side

Thy sons have fainted, they lie at the head of all the streets, as a wild bull in a net: they are full of the fury of the LORD, the rebuke of thy God. Therefore hear now this, thou afflicted, and drunken, but not with wine:
Isaiah 51:20-21

Getting out of prison again was the greatest thing could happen for me. I was entering a new venture. It gave me a chance to help with managing the Tally-Ho. I thought we could really make it work. The restaurant had been there for years. There was already an established clientele. I remembered my family going there to eat. Being a successful businessman had always been in the back of my mind.

When CJ picked me up from the prison, we went directly to the Tally-Ho. We arrived in time to open for breakfast. She began her daily routine. I watched as she made me a special breakfast. There was nothing like having a home cooked meal. In prison, a good meal is a rarity.

I wanted to do right by the business. However, I was also willing to continue committing crimes. This was something I hadn't shared with CJ. I knew she would be against the idea. Crack had become the hottest drug on the market. It seemed to be an easy way to get rich. My thoughts set a trap for me. Money at the Tally-Ho was slow in comparison to drug money.

A friend of mine was in town. He made me a proposition. I thought that if I got a few ounces I would be able to help with the business. Somehow I would have to sneak the money by her. I decided to take my chances with a few ounces. These sold quickly. After this, I picked up a half a key. This was the night I slipped away from CJ. I had arranged a time to meet with my friend. He picked me up down the street from our trailer.

> *The way of peace they know not; and there is no judgment in their goings: they have made them crooked paths: whosoever goeth therein shall not know peace. Therefore is judgment far from us, neither doeth justice overtake us: we wait for light, but behold obscurity; for brightness, but we walk in darkness. We grope for the wall like the blind, and we grope as if we had no eyes: we stumble at noon day as in the night; we are in desolate places as dead men.* Isaiah 59:9

Before going back home, I dropped the drugs off at a safe location. When I got home, I knew I needed a good explanation. The car wasn't in the driveway. It was late and this concerned me. The house was dark. I couldn't find the light switch; eventually, I made my way through the house in the dark. I continued to feel for the light switches, but to no avail.

I thought about one person who would know her whereabouts. Pat lived across the street. It was late, but there was a light on in her trailer. As I knocked on the door I called her name. She answered quickly.

"Pat, have you seen CJ? She's not at home. Where did she go?"

"Are you sure she's not there? Did you check good? Go back home and wait."

When I got back home, I tried my search again. This time, I was careful. I took my time. From the living room, I made my way to the first bedroom. This was Herman's room. I checked the closet. I didn't feel anything. From there I went to the bed. I felt a leg, but it wasn't moving. I moved up to the face. It was CJ. A lot of thoughts were on my mind. Anything could have happened. I hadn't entered the house with her earlier. Did she make it safely into the house? Had someone trailed us home? Had she been robbed? The car was gone. I was worried. When she rose up, I knew she was fine. She didn't want my explanation.

As part of my 'get rich' plan, I got some people to work with me. There were people in my family I wanted to help make money. I didn't know they were using drugs. During my incarceration, a lot of things had changed. Within 24 hours of giving them the package, I went back to check on my money. CJ was with me. She didn't know what was going on. When I checked on the first person, she stated she had been robbed. I didn't believe it. After hearing this, I went to look for the next person. She wasn't there. She drove up before we left her house. When she saw the car, she attempted to back out of the driveway. Before she completed the move, I stopped her. She started crying. She offered a lame explanation.

"I was in a drug house when it was busted. I had to throw the dope away. The police let me leave, but I had to leave the drugs."

She continued crying, but this didn't move me. The only thing that concerned me was my money. Their excuses were part of the cycle. When people use drugs they make excuses for their behavior. This was a cycle I understood.

After these incidents, I had to change my plans. I would have to sell the drugs myself. If I found ten good customers, I could make it. It wasn't long before I sold the package. I narrowed my selection down to five people. My new business started booming. I got comfortable with the fast money. The Tally-Ho became secondary. It was easier to pay someone else to help CJ.

The money was flowing easily. We were enjoying spending it. I still felt CJ had a grudge against me. It was hard to get past this. No matter what I gave her, it wasn't enough. It seemed she wouldn't let go of the embarrassment I had caused her while she was locked up. There were times when she would bring it back up.

Ace was bringing us a lot of goods. He was busted for shoplifting. He called the Tally-Ho to ask for help making bond. He said he would reimburse us. CJ agreed to guarantee the bond. After he was released, he made good on his word by bringing us merchandise. Being around Ace constantly wasn't good for me. It helped to wake up my craving for drugs. One day while I was out taking care of my business, I ran into him. After purchasing some merchandise from him, I took him to get some drugs. After he made the purchase, I took him to get off. Out of nowhere the urge hit me to try it. I felt strong enough to try the drugs. This was supposed to be a one-time occurrence. The drug was so weak, it made me want some more. This was a trap. I bought some more of it. This led me to be gone from the Tally-Ho too long.

When I went back to the restaurant, Ace was with me. CJ detected my condition. She suspected I was high. She started crying.

"I'll be right back. Let me go drop him off."

It was an excuse. I was deceiving myself. The drug wasn't going to let me come directly back. His claws had hooked me again. After this day, I continued trying to hide my drug usage. I fooled myself more than I did her. I was getting off. She was going off. With my niece's help she would track me down.

One night, I was told she had been through Ninth Street with a shotgun, looking for me. When she found me at a relative's house, the gun was on the seat of the car. On another night, I was at one of my cousin's home. When she came into the house, she demanded I leave with her. My cousin pulled a gun out in an attempt to make her leave. This didn't stop her. When we got outside, she threw her pocketbook at me. I merely responded calmly.

"Pick it up. I paid for that."

The next day, my mother received a report of what had happened that night. The report said CJ had clowned for no reason. There was also a message from my aunt.

"Tell her not to ever come back to my house."

In spite of my drug usage, the business continued to prosper. That is until things went wrong. We were invited to a party that night. I was tired. Deciding to spend some quiet time with my wife, we went home. We were just winding down when the call came. When I came to the telephone it was David.

"Buck, man, I have been trying to get in touch with you. My people didn't have anything. I'm doing bad. Do you have a half an ounce?"

"Man, I don't want to talk about all that on the phone. All the mashed potatoes and collard greens are put up."

"Man, please come on. Just bring me an ounce. I'll give you fourteen."

"Where are you, man?"

"Meet me at my store."

CJ was upset.

"You said you were staying at home to relax. Why were you talking all that trash on the phone? Don't go!"

"I'll be right back."

"Buck, don't go out there. You can see him another time. Let him get it somewhere else."

I was the man in this relationship. She couldn't handle me like that. I wasn't going to let her call the shots. My pride wouldn't allow me to listen to her. With my house shoes on, I left the house. I picked up the drugs outside and went off to meet him.

When I arrived at the store, there was no sign of David. I blew my horn. After waiting a minute, I went to a nearby phone. I called CJ. She was still mad, but she gave me the message. David had called to change the location. He wanted to meet me at a nearby shopping plaza.

When I arrived, I scanned the area. There wasn't anything that looked out of place. I spotted his truck. I pulled into an adjacent parking space. There were two people in the truck. I wondered why he had brought someone with him. The windows of the truck were foggy.

Whenever I carried drugs, I kept my doors locked. The person getting out of the truck had a gun. I didn't recognize him. I thought David had set me up to be robbed. About the same time, I saw two other cars trying to block me in. I put my foot on the gas and worked my way from between them. They started shooting. I crouched down in the car and kept getting up. Being caught with an ounce of drugs would lead to a trafficking charge. I needed to get rid of it. They were in high pursuit. I threw the drugs out of the car. I was able to make it to my mother's house. After a hurried stop, I ran around the back of the house and jumped the fence. The neighbors started turning on their lights. I knew my family would be looking, too. At this point, I attempted to surrender. They were screaming at me.

"You made me mess my car up!"

They started hitting me with various objects. It was dark. I couldn't see what hit me. The objects were hard. It felt like flashlights and pistols. I could feel blood running down my neck. I was determined to remain conscious. They took me to one of the police cars. I thought they would only be able to charge me with resisting arrest. My brother came out the house. He saw the blood.

"What's going on? What did you do to my brother?"

Two police officers jumped in front of him.

"Move back sir. This is police business."

From inside the car, I tried to signal him to move back. Police officers went down the street looking for the drugs. Afterwards, they took me to the hospital. I was treated and released in their custody. When I arrived at the jail, I was charged with possession of cocaine. After the preliminaries, I was allowed to call home.

"David set me up."

"I know. Your mother called me."

"CJ, get me out of here. No matter what it takes, get me out of here."

"I'll get you out."

We had a brief conversation before I had to release the line. I knew if there was a way to get me out, CJ would come up with it. I was placed in a holding cell. There was another man in the cell. He provided me with the missing details of my arrest. He had been arrested earlier for a sales case. David was arrested with him. David had been busted with the marked money on him. He didn't trust Benny to hold the money. In exchange for a small piece of the dope, Benny was merely acting as the connection between the parties. It was David's dope.

"They brought both of us down. The last time I saw him, they took him into one of the offices."

The next morning, CJ got me out on bond. We didn't go directly home. We wanted to piece the details together before anyone was aware of my release. David owed me some money. I wanted my money from him. There would be a better chance of collecting the money from him if he didn't know I was free. CJ called him. He attempted to offer explanations. In the end, he agreed to give her the money. She went to his home to pick up the package.

When she returned, she told me about the lame explanation he had offered. He claimed the police had kidnapped him. He also claimed they had stolen his truck. He further explained they had left him handcuffed in the woods. He had no idea where they had gone. Later, they returned with his truck.

CJ took pictures of the bruises and the gash in my head. We checked into a hotel for a few days. I remained out of site. It wouldn't be long before my parole officer found out about the arrest. If he found me, I would be locked up immediately. I began making plans to leave town. When my stitches healed, CJ removed them. We also secured a lawyer.

After taking care of the preliminaries, I left town. Occasionally, I came back to visit CJ. In the beginning, they only lasted a few hours. As time wore on, they became longer. My parole officer wasn't looking for me. There was another person in the office who had taken a personal interest in the case. My old parole officer was actively looking for me. It bordered on harassing CJ. This was the one who referred to me as John Henry. This led to the closing of the Tally-Ho.

Protected by His Grace

And when I passed by thee, and saw thee polluted in thine
own blood, I said unto thee when thou wast in thy blood,
Live; yea, I said unto thee when thou wast in thy blood,
live. Ezekiel 16:6

While running the Tally-Ho, there were many
thieves coming in and out to sell their commodities. Buck
bought me anything I wanted, in an effort to appease me.
Nevertheless, my protesting never stopped. Dee was one
of my friends who were keeping my wardrobe outfitted.
She called me Queen. During this period, Dee had been
hospitalized several times. Each time, she had quickly
recovered. Since the Tally-Ho was closed and she was
out of the hospital, we spent more time together. We were
mostly shoplifting. Again, my role was picking out the
clothes or pulling (distracting the sales person). There was
another person who was with us occasionally, Betty.

In the time of trouble He shall hide me in His
pavilion: in the secret of His tabernacle shall
He hide me; He shall set me up upon the
rock. Psalm 27:5

One day when I was taking Dee stealing, she got
into a physical confrontation with her boyfriend. It
happened in Buck's car. We were driving through the East
Wynnton area. Buck was still out of town in hiding. She
wanted her boyfriend to stay behind, as we went on the
mission. She was concerned that the way he was dressed
would draw unneeded attention in the better stores. He

wasn't opposed to staying behind, but he wanted her to get some money from me. He wanted to purchase him a sack of heroin. She refused to ask me for the money and they started arguing. The argument escalated, forcing me to stop in the middle of the street. A fight ensued in the back seat of the car. One of them broke a pint gin bottle in the midst of the fight. He began to beat her with the bottle. He walked off leaving her lying in the street. She crawled tediously back into the front seat of the car. After he walked off, a lady watching nearby approached the car.

She said, "Wait Charlotte! Let me get a towel. She's bleeding."

My children were with my mother and needed to be picked up, before I went home. After making sure Dee was going to survive, it was only then that my thoughts turned to AIDS. These thoughts hadn't crossed my mind before this time. My only concern had been assuring my friend wouldn't bleed to death. Once this was assured, the amount of blood in the car concerned me.

While in prison, we had been given AIDS education. At the time, I really didn't listen. This disease happened to other peopled. It happened to certain kinds of people, homosexuals, hemophiliacs, and IV (intravenous) drug users. They were at high risk for infection. I didn't fit the stereotype. Consequently, I didn't think it was necessary to listen to the information. As a partner to an IV drug user, I was at risk. I was in denial like so many other people. My earlier relationships hadn't left me risk free. There was plenty of risk. Sleeping with only one person can put you at risk. Neither of my past relations could make this claim. They took pride in this fact; they had numerous paramours.

The only thing I remembered from the presentation was bleach and gloves were needed before attempting to clean a blood spill. From the counter in the examination room, I grabbed a pair of gloves. The car would need to be cleaned carefully.

Buck remained out of town in hiding and we seldom saw each other. One day, Dee and I decided to go to the city where he was hiding. This wasn't just for a visit. This was a good place for a shoplifting trip. We picked up Buck before we got started. Everything started out going well, but as usual, we got greedy. Dee was an excellent thief, but she had started slipping. When we got to the last store, Buck said he was tired and didn't want to go in. This is the only time I can remember him not wanting to take something. This should have been enough to change our minds.

We proceeded into the store without him. Dee picked up some garments. In her haste, she missed the buzzers. As we were leaving the store, the alarm went off. We had to run to the car. A Good Samaritan saw what had happened and jumped into his car to follow us. I drove faster than I ever had before. I was running lights and cutting in and out of traffic. The man was following right behind me. We traveled for several blocks, through congested traffic at this pace. He was determined to catch the car. Finally, he saw a policeman and flagged him down. When he stopped to explain to the police officer why he was chasing us, we were able to escape. I had a spare tag in the trunk. Pulling onto a side street, we found an empty house where the tag could be changed. This was enough excitement for one day. We were ready to drop Buck off and return to Columbus. My sentence was waiting for me if I was caught. A few weeks after this incident, he moved back to Columbus.

For years, I had been co-dependent, trying to make Buck stop using drugs. There was a constant fear he would overdose. If he was away from home for an extended period, I would go looking for him and bring him home. As he became accustomed to this practice, he learned to expect my arrival. One night he stayed out all night getting high. There was no doubt, where he was, at his mother's house. All night long, I called, trying to get him to come home. Finally, I decided to make him either paranoid enough or mad enough to come home. This was sure to get a reaction from him.

"If you don't come home, I'm going to call your parole officer and tell him how to find you."

This worked. Within ten minutes, he was coming through the door. Buck wasn't prone to hit me. He has a rather even disposition and it takes a lot to make him mad. My mouth had provoked him to this point. When he came in the door, I was sitting on the sofa, anxiously waiting. I hadn't thought about what would happen once he got there. When he rushed at me with his hand positioned to strike me. With reflex action, my body balled up into a knot. There was no way I was going to let him hit me with those big hands. His hands are twice the size of my hands. Out of fear, I kicked out of my fetal position, prepared to run. This caught him off guard and a 6'2", 225 lb. Buck fell backward onto the glass coffee table breaking it. My feet ran down the hall and out of a side door. Behind me, there was the sound of breaking glass. After getting up, he began breaking other things in the house.

With lightening speed, I ran across the street to Pat's house. Buck was right behind me. We both went straight to her bedroom. She was sitting on the side of the bed. Like a professional referee, she went to work.

"Calm down! What's wrong? Have a seat."

Since he hadn't hit me yet, I sat down on the bed. I was comfortable he wouldn't hit me.

Again, Pat instructed, "Buck sit down."

He responded, "I can't."

She asked him why and he turned around. He was wearing his navy blue and burgundy velour Christian Dior jogging suit. A chunk of meat was gapping through the cut in the back of his pants and he was bleeding. He said he was going over to his mother's to get the wound bandaged. After he left in his car, I followed him. His mother, sister, and brother-in-law were standing outside the house when I arrived. His sister was taking him to the hospital emergency room in Phenix City for treatment. His mother and sister were angry with me.

"You could have killed my son! I can't put a bandage on that! Take him to the hospital!"

There was no response from me; she wasn't talking to me. She was expressing her anger at me and instructing his sister to take him to the hospital. Anyway, Mama had trained me not to disrespect my elders.

In my mind the response was, "If he had hit me with that fist, he would have killed me. If you had sent him home, none of this would have happened."

When he got in the car with her and her husband, I got in with him. When we entered the emergency room, I walked to the desk with him, answering all the questions they asked him. When they called him to the back room for treatment, I went quietly with him. While the nurse stitched him up, I watched quietly. Through the whole thing, Buck spoke as little as possible. He was no longer high or angry with me. He remained quiet so no one else would know. They were angry, but he had already forgiven me. When he left the hospital, the nurse instructed him to see a doctor in a few days to have the stitches removed. In five days, Dr. CJ removed the stitches. It was part of the cycle.

After one of our numerous breakups, Buck went to Atlanta with Herb. Somehow, I learned he was there. This was too much for me to bear. My fear of him overdosing escalated. The drugs were more potent in Atlanta. They were also more readily available. Off to Atlanta I went. I stopped at one of his favorite drug spots. They told me that he hadn't been in the neighborhood. After riding through the neighborhood several times, I stopped to use a pay telephone. Buck turned down the street that intersected the street I was parked on. He didn't stop, but he had seen me. The speed of the car verified this fact. He was not getting away that easily. With the determination of a mule, I jumped into my car. I chased him across town. Eventually, he gave up.

As it was getting close to two years that I had been on parole, my parole officer told me she was recommending my sentence be commuted. This was something I had never heard of and never thought was possible. In my amazement, the part about this being a recommendation wasn't heard. With all of my gratitude and jubilation, I almost blew this recommendation before the process was complete.

Since it was extremely difficult for me to see Buck with two parole officers checking on us, I thought it would be much easier if we physically moved the trailer. In a couple of days, the trailer was moved to different street and painted a different color. This didn't stop my paranoia that they were going to catch us. Buck would go to bed and leave me up worrying about the parole officers.

By God's grace, my sentence was commuted. It took several months for the process to be completed. Before it was finalized, my stealing escapades escalated.

Protected by His Grace: Flip Side

Taste and see that the LORD is good. Oh, the joys of those who trust in Him!
Psalm 34:8 (NLT)

After I was busted, I went to Cincinnati, Ohio. When I called home, CJ told me about the incident with Dee. I wanted to know why she was driving my car. It didn't make me happy knowing that the altercation had occurred in my car. I didn't mind Dee being in the car. However, I didn't approve her riding him in the car. I had known him for years. He wasn't someone I wanted hanging around my wife. He couldn't be trusted.

"Did he disrespect you?"

"No!"

It alleviated some of the tension, but I was still mad.

"Why weren't you driving your car? Did you take him stealing with you?"

She just dismissed everything as if it was under control. In the back of my mind, it was added worry. I left home because things were going wrong. In my absence, they were still going wrong. She was falling in love with stealing.

Things weren't going right where I was either. My connection hadn't come through. After a few weeks, we came back to Columbus. There was another person who had left town with me. I was medicating while I was gone, but not on a regular basis. When we got back, I started medicating strongly. She started nagging strongly.

One night, I was medicating heavily. I needed a comfortable place to get high. I could always go to my mother's house. I couldn't go home though. CJ wasn't going to allow me any peace if I tried. She was good at blowing my high. All night long, I got high. All night, CJ called me. That morning, she got my attention and blew my high in the process.

She told me she was going to call my parole officer. They were already looking for me. I hurried out of the house. Once outside, I jumped into my car. This threat needed to be straightened out. This was out of bounds. This threat went too far. The police were never to have anything to do with our disagreements or our relationship. She knew she had crossed the line. Instantly, she had my attention. She had been working on me all night. I rushed home.

A man's pride shall bring him low: but honour
shall uphold the humble in spirit.
Proverbs 29:23

When I got there, she was sitting on the sofa. There was no reason for her to be afraid of me. I had never beaten her. It wasn't in my nature. I was going to poke her with my finger. When I came in, I guess she reverted to the past. There was a glass table between the door and the sofa. I moved in front of the sofa. The table was behind me. I was angry and my voice was somewhat elevated. It was louder than normal. The drugs were still in my system. She had her legs drawn up under her. She pushed at me with her foot. I stumbled backward and sat on the table. This cracked the table and the table cracked me. She took off running. I walked quickly behind her.

She ran across the street to Pat's house and went straight to her bedroom. I followed close behind her. It was obvious to Pat something was wrong. Pat tried to console me.

"Wait Buck! What's wrong? Sit down let me talk to you."

This wasn't possible. I was conscious of an opening in the back of my warm-up suit. When I reached behind me, I realized I had been cut. There was blood running down my leg. Pat talked to us briefly and I left. I got in my car and drove quickly to my mother's house.

When I arrived, I asked my Mama to look at the cut. My sister looked at the cut, too. My sister was prone to blow things out of proportion. As usual, she made my injury seem worse than it was.

"You've got to have stitches. How did this happen?"

"I fell back on the coffee table. I was arguing with Charlotte about putting the folks on me."

They agreed. I needed to go to the hospital for stitches. With the warrant out on me, I couldn't go to a hospital in Columbus. It was too risky. Someone might recognize me. Consequently, I went to hospital in Phenix City, AL. I called a friend and asked if I could use her address with a false name. By this time, CJ arrived. My brother-in-law and sister took me to the hospital. I was accompanied by CJ. The emergency room wasn't crowded. They treated me immediately. They gave me about eight stitches. CJ was in there when they sewed me up. My injury wasn't serious. However, it was in an awkward place.

After they finished treating the wound, I went back to my mother's house. That night, I went home. We didn't discuss what had happened earlier. When it was time for the stitches to be removed, CJ took them out. It was the second time she removed my stitches.

When pride comes, then comes disgrace, but
with humility comes wisdom.
Proverbs 11:2 (NIV)

My friends didn't understand why I kept going back to her. She nagged me all the time. There was one thing I knew. Even in the nagging, I could learn something from her. She had my best interest at heart. They had selfish reasons for wanting me to stay in the streets.

A few days later, I went to Atlanta with Herb. He was having problems at home, too. We decided to go to Atlanta to get a break for a few days. This would also give me a chance to get away from CJ and my problems.

She kept turning up everywhere I went. This was no different. I was driving down the street when I spotted her. Herb may have seen her first. How did she know I was in Atlanta? At the time, I was on a mission. The drugs were already in my system. I was trying to increase my medication. It was better for me to shake her off my trail. If I drove fast enough, maybe she would give up. With foot pressed on the gas petal, I sped off. She was right behind me. Herb thought our trip was coming to an end.

A wrathful man stirreth up strife: but he that is
slow to anger appeaseth strife.
Proverbs 15:18

It was better for me stop and talk to her. If we kept driving at this pace we were going to get a ticket or end up wrecking the cars. Herb wasn't in agreement. He was cursing.

"Man, don't go talk to her."

I ignored his words. It was easier to pull over. When I pulled into a parking lot, she pulled up behind me. As I was exiting my car, I called out to her. I tried to sound angry.

"CJ, what do you want?"

Her cousin was in the car with her. As I approached the car, I heard them talking.

"He's not mad. He called me CJ. If he was mad, he would have said Charlotte."

I wanted to be mad with her. The truth was I just wasn't mad. Even with the drugs in my system, I wanted to be with her. It had been several days since I had seen her. I missed her. After a brief conversation, I followed my heart. Herb could drive my car back to Columbus. I was going with my wife. I walked back to my car and informed Herb of my decision. I got in the car with her. The next day, we drove back to Columbus. The reconciliation didn't last long. In a few days, I was back at my old tricks. She responded the same way. The cycle continued to spin.

Feel What I Feel

Feel what I feel my friend,
I'm hurting and it's destroying me from within
I want you to feel what I feel
Even if it destroys me in the end

Feel what I feel my friend
Feel my pain, feel my hurt
There has to be a way for this pain to end
Prove that you care about me through thick and thin

You say you love me
You say that for me you care
Why then can't you feel what I feel?

Can't you feel what I feel?
If it's true that you love me
Why is this pain so real that I feel?

Dear friend, please feel what I feel
My heart won't you help heal
My friend this has to end
If you feel what I feel
We prevail in the end

Dear God, just let him feel what I feel.
Tell me the pain isn't real.
Because You feel what I feel.

Feel What I Feel

The LORD nurses them when they are sick
and eases their pain and discomfort. Psalm 41:3 (NLT)

The first of many dreams came while I was serving my prison sentence. Several years later, there was another troubling dream. I was at Buck's mother's house. It wasn't the house she lived in at the time. However, she lives in this house today. Before the dream, I had never seen this house. I was lying on the floor. From beneath the door I could see outside. In front of the house, Ace and Buck were standing near Buck's car. Police were everywhere. They were searching the car. When I woke up, I asked Buck where he was going.

"I'm going to work."

"Who's going with you?"

"I'm going to stop by Ace's house."

"Please don't go to work today."

"Why?"

"You're going to get caught if you do."

"Ah man."

He kept preparing to go. As he was dressing, I continued to beg him to change his plans. Ace had only been out of prison for about a week. I called him at his mother's house.

"You just got out of prison. Why are you stealing again? Don't go stealing with Buck. If you do, you're going to get caught. Don't put your mother through this again. Give her a break."

He listened to me. He always listened to me. Nevertheless, he never headed my warnings. When Buck left the house, I still wasn't satisfied. In my car, I drove to Ace's house. They had been delayed in leaving. Buck had to knock the monkey off his back before they could leave. I pleaded with both of them not to go. In the end, I got mad. As they drove off, I yelled behind them.

"Don't call me when you get caught."

When I returned home, I called Betty on the telephone.

"They are going to get caught today."

"Don't worry about it. If they won't listen, let them go on."

When I got the telephone call, I was still talking to Betty. In addition to this, I was also relaxing my hair.

"CJ, you need to come pick me up. I can't drive my car. They are looking for it."

"Where's Ace?"

"I'm not sure. He jumped out of the car to run when they got behind us."

"Why did he do that? He knows he can't run."

"We tried to throw them off by throwing clothes out the car. They may have caught him."

He gave me directions to pick him up. He was waiting in a hospital emergency room. After washing the relaxer from my hair, I wrapped my hair in a towel. As I drove through several counties, I saw law enforcement officers everywhere. They were waiting for him to head back to Columbus. I drove carefully. When I arrived at the hospital, Buck walked out. It wasn't time for me to rub it in. He took me to where his car was parked. I got behind the wheel. He took my car and followed me. We didn't head for Columbus. Instead, we headed for Atlanta. After driving approximately fifty miles, we detoured back towards Columbus.

This also started a cycle for Ace. He understood the cycle. He's never broken it. On several occasions after he was released from prison, he ran into me. The next day, he would be arrested. I was a warning to him. He would tell me.

"Every time I see you, I go jail. Don't warn me."

He smiled when he said it. I warned him every time I saw him. Today, I'm still warning him.

It started as frustration. In the end, it was more desperation. The cycles were constantly spinning. It seemed they would never end. We kept repeating the same mistakes. I was tired of our lifestyle. Buck was also wearing my patience out - that's if I had any patience. I was hurting. The pain was deep and getting deeper. Why didn't he feel my pain? Why didn't he feel what I felt? He said he loved me. What kind of love caused such deep pain?

I wanted him to feel the pain. It started out with a ride to the corner. Once there, I parked the car. With the stereo playing, I waited for time to pass. When I returned home, I offered no explanation for my trips. This didn't seem to dig deep enough. He was suspicious of the trips. Still, he didn't feel my pain. He didn't understand the frustration that was developing. He didn't understand the turmoil. It was horrible wondering when he would come home. I was determined; he was going to feel my pain.

There had to be a way to get through to him. Defeat wasn't an option for me. I came up with my plan. Two could play this game. That's when I started stealing without him. Anybody else would do. We passed each other in the streets. I pretended I didn't see him. The second part of my plan involved a waiting game. At night, I was going to be the last person to arrive home. He was going to look for me.

My plan seemed to be working. I saw worry in his eyes. In the middle of the day, he would return home. When he came in the door, I headed out the door. It didn't matter where I went. I was trying to break the cycle at any cost. Buck started calling Mama for help. He wanted her to talk to me. He hoped she would be able to get me to stay home. This didn't work. I was hurting and I wanted him to feel the pain.

Most of the time, I went stealing with Dee. This was on the days when she wasn't sick. The first time she was hospitalized, I was still running the Tally-Ho. From her hospital room, she called me.

"Queen, come up here. I have some things for you."

When I arrived at the hospital, she presented me with the items. In her illness, she had found time to work. She had been shopping at the hospital gift shop. I paid her for the package.

"O LORD," I prayed, "have mercy on me. Heal me, for I have sinned against you." But my enemies say nothing but evil about me. "How soon will he die and be forgotten?" they ask. They visit me as if they are my friends, but all the while they gather gossip, and when they leave, they spread it everywhere. All who hate me whisper about me, imagining the worst for me. "Whatever he has, it is fatal," they say. "He will never get out of that bed!"
Psalm 41:4-8 (NLT)

The next time she was in the hospital, it wasn't that simple. The telephone call disturbed me greatly.

"Queen, why are they treating me like this?"

"What's wrong?"

"People are passing by my room peeping at me. They think I don't see them. They even come from other floors. They act like I'm some kind of freak. I don't know what they are telling people I have. I don't have AIDS."

As she spoke, tears swelled up in my eyes. My voice choked. I could visualize the people looking at her. I felt her pain. It reminded me of a familiar pain, my own. It was more painful than I could bear. There was no way I would be able to visit her and remain calm. During her hospital stays, I would never be able to visit her again.

One day when I took Dee stealing, things went wrong almost immediately. The assistant manager was looking strange, although nothing had been stolen. Dee had stolen something from the store on the previous day. I wasn't with her. Nevertheless, I had purchased most of the items from her. As Dee was looking around the store, I exchanged one of the items for my correct size.

Dee walked up to me and said, "Queen, I'm going to get you a mink coat."

Something didn't feel right.

I told her, "Don't do it. I think we need to get out of here."

Walking away, she said, "No Queen! I'm going to get you a mink coat."

The assistant manager looked directly in my face. Something was wrong with the look she was giving me. As I headed towards the door, the assistant manager paged the manager to come to the department. On his way there, he passed by me. I spoke to him and calmly made my way to the car. Looking through my rear view mirror, I observed that both the manager and assistant manager had walked out of the store to look for me. They were looking directly at me. My car was parked only two parking spaces from the front door of the store. They turned and went back inside the store. They hadn't seen me. Again, God had spared me. The final paper hadn't been signed commuting my sentence. If I had been caught, there were still over twelve years remaining on my sentence.

Looking for a better place to watch for Dee, I drove up a hill. At the top of the hill, I parked in a place where the store could be observed through the shrubbery. After waiting for several minutes, it was apparent that she wasn't coming out. I couldn't risk staying parked near the store. They might search the area.

I called someone else to come to the store and check on her. When he arrived at the store, the police were bringing Dee out. Apparently, the theft on the previous day had been uncovered. He overheard her explaining that her disease made her do this. After her release, she told me about the arrest.

"I told them I had AIDS and was going to bite them. They didn't believe me. I was joking about having the virus."

By the time Dee arrived at the jail, the arrangements had been made for a bondsman to get her out. The bondsman was willing to allow us to bring the money back for the bond fee. When I picked Dee up, we did just enough stealing to get the money to pay him. Dee had actually been sick for some time. This was just one of the few days she felt well enough to go out.

On another day, we went to a grocery store. Dee had picked up several whole New York Strips. Buck was at the checkout talking to someone. She walked to the front of the store. She was acting disoriented. The meat was exposed. I was standing outside the store when I observed an employee in the process of locking the door.

I was able to get inside before the task was finished. When they apprehended her, I commented that she appeared disoriented. I agreed to purchase the meat for her. They agreed to let her go. They didn't know we were together. It cost me eighty dollars, but I liked steak.

Once while at our trailer, she walked off the side of the steps rather than walking down the steps. This was before we moved the trailer. We couldn't understand why or how she had fallen. She had fallen flat on her face, but she wasn't hurt in the fall. She didn't know what had happened. Subsequently, her memory became affected by what was going on with her.

In the meantime, my marriage was beginning to deteriorate rapidly. Things had reached a point where Buck and I no longer spent any time together. Whenever I thought he was coming home, I would leave. I was tired of living the way we had been living for years. At night, sleep wouldn't come.

Late one night, I observed a couple parking a car in a lot across from our trailer. This lot served as the parking lot for the trailer park's business office. The office had been closed for several hours. After parking the car, they walked down the street and out of my sight. My thoughts immediately went to parole officers. I went to each window in the trailer trying to recapture my view of them. My search included trying to catch a glimpse of these two people hiding behind one of the neighboring trailers. Buck went to bed, leaving me watching through the windows. I waited until the couple returned to my view, about 8:00 the next morning. As they drove off in the car, the realization came; they had their own secrets. All night long, it had been apparent; I was tripping. I just didn't realize the extent of the trip. For hours, I had been looking out the window. Normally, the high didn't last this long.

There was money, there were drugs, there were clothes, but they weren't free. The cost they extracted was my peace.

I said, I will take heed to my ways, that I sin not with my tongue: I will keep my mouth with a bridle, while the wicked is before me. I was dumb with silence, I held my peace, even from good; and my sorrow was stirred. My heart was hot within me, while I was musing the fire burned: then spake I with my tongue,
Psalm 39:1-3

Looking over my shoulders for police officers and parole officers was getting tiresome. My sentence had been commuted, but still the paranoia of police officers and parole officers remained. Buck didn't share my feelings. My frustration with his drug usage was escalating. My desire was for him to feel the pain I had felt for years, while he was out getting high, the pain of being a second love. Drugs were always his priority. I knew how to compete with a woman, but I didn't know how to compete with a spirit of addiction. Our days of even having polite conversations passed. He went on his mission and I went on mine.

As Dee became sicker, Betty and I went stealing together. We bought cocaine and marijuana after we peddled our goods. This began a pattern that lasted for a couple of months. She lived in another nearby trailer park. Sharing whatever we had, we would split the money and drugs in half. She smoked her cocaine in cigarettes. My joints were sprinkled with cocaine. Usually, after we each smoked one, I would go home. If Buck was there, this wasn't an option. Once I returned home, Betty and I would talk on the telephone or should I say we tripped (experienced drug related paranoia) on the telephone.

Betty was hiding from her parole officer, too. While I was no longer on parole, the parole officers were still looking for Buck. This didn't seem to bother him, but this stayed on my mind constantly.

The cocaine made us extremely paranoid. Most of the paranoia centered on fear of parole officers. Sometimes we worried about hidden cameras and police officers. However, mostly it was the parole officers. Whenever we were high, we imagined the parole officers were at the door. The craziest part of this was we were at least six blocks apart. We would hold the telephone, speaking only occasionally.

If I responded, "I hear somebody. I'm going to sit here quietly with the lights out."

Over six blocks away, Betty would respond, "I hear them outside my door, too. I'm going to do the same thing. I'll cut the lights out. If they don't hear anything maybe they'll go away."

There was no sense of peace in our home. In the middle of the night, I would call Mama or my friend Esther and tell them how troubled my mind was. There was no understanding of what was wrong with me. The money wasn't helping and the marijuana wasn't making me laugh anymore. They told me to read the Bible. Through my tears, I tried to read. It wasn't working because it seemed the words wouldn't come together to make a complete sentence. They told me to pray. What was I supposed to say? They told me I needed to come home. Where was home? How was I supposed to get there? It seemed I was a long way from home. I didn't know how to get back. Nothing was alleviating my misery. My antics continued.

In the day of my trouble I sought the Lord: my
sore ran in the night, and ceased not: my
soul refused to be comforted. I remembered

God, and was troubled: I complained, and my spirit was overwhelmed. Thou holdeth mine eyes waking: I am so troubled that I cannot speak. Psalm 77:2-4

Things were getting worse. Dee had been sick for a while and the rumors were flying. It became apparent; she was seriously ill. She denied the rumor that she had AIDS, telling me once she had been misdiagnosed. As time passed, I became more afraid she was going to die. I didn't want to deal with the pain. There was enough pain in my own life. I didn't need to feel the pain she was feeling. I couldn't take anymore. Deciding I couldn't handle the possibility of her death, my decision was to limit my telephone calls to Dee. This resulted in my hanging out with Betty regularly. The rumors about Dee began to escalate. Actually, I never heard anyone talk about her illness. She told me people were spreading the rumors. My hopes were that somehow these rumors were wrong. Dee couldn't be dying from AIDS. There had to be a mistake. This couldn't be true. These were just cruel heartless rumors.

Feel What I Feel: The Flip Side

If he take him another wife; her food, her raiment, and her duty of marriage, shall he not diminish. Exodus 21:10

CJ was in her own world. I couldn't understand what was happening with her. My conscious was working overtime. My mind was also working overtime. I was trying to figure her out, but at the same time I was concentrating on my next mission. My monkey was also requiring more food (medication).

Without her nagging me to kick the drugs, this gave me more time to indulge. It also increased the length of time I went without taking a break from using them. This increased my tolerance for the drugs. It required bigger quantities to keep the monkey checked. CJ needed my attention. I wasn't ready to change. I knew in order for me to kick, I had to stay home. This would mean being sick for several days. I had done this several times in the past. Each time, she remained by my side until I made it through the sickness. I wasn't kicking for myself. In an effort to appease her, I endured the sickness. It was never going to last if I didn't do it for myself. At this point, she wasn't asking me to quit. She was doing something new. This threw me off course.

Her nagging gave my life balance. It also gave me hope; one day, I would kick the habit permanently. It was a dangerous game, but the cycle was out of control. Medicating gave me an excuse not to deal with my problems. When the medication wore off, the problems returned. Using the drugs created additional problems. There was guilt on top of the problems. There was only one way to alleviate the guilt, medicate again. This kept the cycle going.

It wasn't hard to figure out what she was doing. She was stealing. I knew the people she was hustling with. What bothered me was I didn't know the rest of the story. She had always been limited in her drug usage. It was almost casual. She smoked marijuana and drank champagne. Her partners were into a different type of drug usage. I didn't think they could influence her. However, I knew the kind of games they played. This concerned me. She might take stealing to a new level. They were people who had been my partners on other missions. The money was also a concern. I didn't know how they were splitting the take. This might not be done fairly. I didn't want anybody to take advantage of her.

If she was going stealing, I preferred she go with me. This would keep all the money in our house. It had worked well for us in the past. The house would be taken care of and I would have plenty of money for the drugs. CJ is good at managing money. If she was working with me, I would have someone to bail me out if I got in trouble. The guys I was working with were looking out for themselves. It was fine for us to take the lick together. When it came time for me to get out of jail, I didn't want to trust them with my freedom. I could trust her. If something went wrong, she would find a way to correct it. I missed the security. I missed the closeness. I missed my partner and my wife.

One day, I was getting ready to go to work. Ace and I had this prearranged. When CJ woke up, she started nagging. My monkey was nagging, too. CJ had dreamed I was going to get caught this day. My monkey told me to ignore her. The monkey won the debate. We went ahead with our plan.

We made it to our destination and we proceeded to the inside of the store. We completed the sting without any trouble. As we were leaving the store, we both had a trash bag full of goods. I saw two men coming up behind us. They were moving fast and purposefully.

"Ace, we have company."

We made it to the car. The key was ready for a speedy getaway. When they saw us get in the car, they radioed for backup. We had planned to run if anything went wrong. We planned to meet at the nearest fast food restaurant. This was the way I headed. I saw a police car coming towards us. Ace panicked.

"Let me out."

Hoping to distract or delay them, he threw the bags out of the car. As a last resort, he got out of the car and started running. I sped off and made it to a nearby hospital parking lot. The tag on the car wasn't the car's real tag. I changed the tag on the car back to the proper one. The fake tag was ditched in a nearby sewer. Inside the hospital, I was forced to call CJ. I needed her help. She was going to argue, but I had to endure it. I watched from the hospital window for her arrival. Police vehicles raced past looking for me. CJ arrived first.

We were married, but she acted as if we were strangers. She didn't want me to touch her. Sometimes, she slept in the living room. There were other times when she slept in her clothes. Most of the time, she was at the far side of the bed with an invisible wall between us. I tried to be courteous and kind. I offered her gifts. She continued to take the merchandise. If I had something I thought she would like, I brought it home. When I showed her what I brought her, she wouldn't make any comments.

There was no gratitude, no thank you. If I put clothes in the closet or on the bed, I knew she would choose what she wanted.

The drugs had my mind cloudy. When I was high, I didn't think the relationship was in trouble. After the drugs wore off, reality set in. There were holes in our relationship in need of major repairs, but how could I repair them with the monkey on my back? The drugs said everything was going to work out. The relationship wasn't in trouble. I couldn't feel what she was feeling. The drugs masked and clouded my own feelings.

One day, I came home early. CJ was at the trailer, smoking with Betty. I could smell the cocaine in the marijuana. I decided I needed help to get things straightened out between us. CJ would listen to her mother. At least, I was hoping she would listen. Maybe, Ma' Evelyn could help me. Hesitantly, I called her. It had occurred to me to call her sooner. However, I didn't want her to know everything going on between us.

"Ma' Evelyn, I usually don't call you to talk about our situation. I feel this is very important. CJ is out there deeply with cocaine."

"Oh Buck! Where is she now?"

"She's over to Betty's house."

After we hung up, I felt guilty. She didn't know anything about what we had been doing. She knew one thing, not to accept anything from us. The guilt lingered with me for a minute. Still, I felt I needed to do something. I called Betty's house and asked to speak to CJ.

I don't remember what happened after the telephone call. Sometime later, CJ came home. After this day, I never discussed this incident with Ma' Evelyn again. Nothing changed with CJ. She continued hanging out with her friends. I continued to medicate my feelings.

Married to the Backslider

I will heal their backsliding; I will love thee freely:
for mine anger is turned away from him. Hosea 14:4

One morning, my mind began to dwell on Dee. I decided to call her. When she answered the telephone, she told me she had been waiting for me to call her. She asked me to hold on while she hung up from her boyfriend, on the other line. This in itself was strange and troubled me. He was the person who had beaten her in Buck's car. When she returned to the line, she informed me her illness had caused her to forget my telephone number. I told her I would get Buck to bring her a telephone that could be programmed to call me by dialing only one number. At this point, she made the announcement that rang in my ears for days.

"I want you to know that I am HIV Positive and I'm going to die within the next two weeks."

At this time, I was concerned about her soul, but I wasn't worthy to discuss Jesus or the blood He shed for the remission of our sins. She had never been told I was a backslider. This was a part of my life I was desperately trying to hide. There was never any doubt in my mind; God was real. The Holy Spirit talked to me. He was constantly warning me. Every time I had gotten in trouble, His voice had warned me. Yet, I could only call Him 'Something.' This was because I wasn't ready to submit my will to Him. No matter how bad things got for me, no matter how many times I had been counted out, He had always pulled me out. I wasn't worthy to talk about Him. As a result, I was faced with what was really the biggest spiritual challenge of my life. Dee had just said she was dying. I didn't want her to go hell, but I wasn't worthy to tell her how to be "saved". There had to be a way to make sure she was "saved" without me having to call His name.

For I am ready to be offered, and the time of my departure is at hand. I have fought a good fight, I have finished my course, I have kept the faith: henceforth is laid up for me a crown of righteousness, which the Lord, the righteous judge, shall give me at that day: and not to me only, but unto all them that love His appearing. 2 Timothy 4:7-8

Almost without breathing, I said, "If you feel like that, what have you done about it?"

Dee responded, "I have been praying."

I didn't even feel worthy to say pray and so I responded, "What did you say?"

As if somehow understanding what I was trying not to say, she indulged me in a very foolish conversation. Wanting to be sure she had indeed prayed a PRAYER OF TRUE REPENTANCE, after each statement, I asked an additional question.

"And how did you do that?"

After answering all the questions to my satisfaction, she told me, "I've fought a good fight. I'm tired. I've been dreaming about my grandmother. She was in a room and there were many steps leading to the room. I wanted to leave the room, but my grandmother begged me to stay. She told me if I left, I wouldn't be able to come back in. I didn't listen and I went out of the room. There were a lot of steps to get back to the door leading to the room, but I wanted to get back in so bad. I kept knocking on the door.

Someone opened the door and said, 'He said knock and the door shall be opened.' I'm ready to die. I just don't want to die alone. I know I've done a lot of things wrong."

Sickness reminded me of my own struggle. I was afraid of people who were terminally ill. I was afraid their pain would cause me to relive my own. That evening, the conversation with Dee was shared with Buck. Dee lingered on my mind all day, but I wasn't ready to deal with the possibility of her death.

For mine iniquities are gone over mine head: as an heavy burden they are too heavy for me. My wounds stink and are corrupt because of my foolishness. I am troubled; I am bowed down greatly; I go mourning all the day long.
Psalm 38:4-6

I spent the next day getting high with Betty. We were afraid Dee was dying. We were trying to numb the pain. We didn't want to be alone. That afternoon, Dee's mother called Betty's house to tell us she had passed. She told us Dee died lying in her arms. Dee was in pain. In spite of this, after she took her last breath, a smile came across her face. The painkiller didn't work. God's grace worked.

There would be several days before Dee was buried. Betty and I were too upset to go stealing, but we had to find a way to keep the painkiller going. The devil was having a field day with our minds. For me, he was trying to destroy me with guilt. Each day was requiring more efforts to deal with the pain. We never managed to get high enough.

Betty and I drove to the funeral together, torn by our grief. On the outside we were dressed immaculately, looking as if we had everything neatly tied together in a picture perfect package; inside we were more like used tissue paper. While the policeman led the funeral procession, we were drinking beer and smoking a joint.

After the funeral, Betty said she needed to go to church the next day. Agreeing this was a good idea, I told her I would go with her. We had no real idea what church we were going to, but we were going.

The next morning, I got up and put on my beige Harve' Bernard suit and a Blue Fox coat. On the outside everything was in place. On the inside, everything was in disarray. I didn't just feel cheap; I felt like trash. Buck was lying in bed looking at me. He knew this was too early for me to be going stealing. The stores wouldn't open until 1:00. The look in his eyes was asking, "Where are you going?" The look beaming back from my eyes told him not to verbalize the question. I left the house without saying one word to him. My anger about our lifestyles had reached the brink.

> *Oh, that you would listen to His voice today! The Lord says, don't harden your hearts as Israel did at Meribah, and as they did at Massah in the wilderness. For there your ancestors tried My patience; they courted My wrath though they had seen My many miracles.* Psalm 95:7b-9 (NLT)

Betty and I rode around the city looking for a church to attend. After stopping at a couple of churches and ruling them out as possibilities, we ended up at my mother's church, my old church. There was a new pastor there. As we walked around the side of the church, unexpectedly, the familiar voice of 'Something' spoke to me.

"It's over."

Married to the Backslider: The Flip Side

Turn, O backsliding children, saith the LORD; for I am married unto you: and I will take you one of a city, and two of a family, and I will bring you to Zion: Jeremiah 3:14

It had been some time since I had seen Dee. Several things had been said about Dee that didn't add up. I had heard rumors, but I didn't believe them. We had been friends for years. There was no reason to believe the rumors. She hadn't shared this with me. The rumors were dismissed.

When she walked off the porch at our house, I was concerned about her. She was always a professional thief. It was apparent something was wrong with her. She was making mistakes that were out of her character.

We went by Dee's house one day to see her. She was sick and confined to the bed. Dee told us the doctors had made a mistake.

"They thought I had AIDS. They found out that's not what's wrong with me. They are running some other test on me."

While we were at the house, another friend called. She asked to speak to me.

"Buck don't get too close to the bed. Don't get too close to the phone."

This was just another rumor. What she said didn't make any sense. She had asked to speak to me. This was the only reason I was holding the telephone. Dee was able to shake the sickness off and went back to work. It wasn't long before she was sick again. She continued to abuse drugs.

One day when I came in from work, CJ gave me the news. It was true. Dee had confirmed she had AIDS. She had a question for me.

"Have you ever shared a needle with her?"

"No!"

Truthfully, I wasn't sure. In the early 80's it was common to share needles. There were two people who CJ knew had been involved with Dee.

"Have you ever shared a needle with either of them?"

"No!"

I was searching my memory, trying to remember. Had I been exposed? Had I shared a needle with someone who had been exposed? I wasn't sure. All day long, I thought about Dee. Most of the time, we bought new works (needles). In times of emergency, we used bleach. Before we used bleach, we used alcohol. Nonetheless, there had been other times. These were the times I was trying to remember. I didn't tell CJ, I was worried. There was a lot to think about. My friends were on my mind. Had they been exposed? And there was the issue of sex partners. Sometimes it seemed like a family affair. Some women had slept with most of the guys in the neighborhood. When one relationship ended, it was common for them to become involved with one of the guy's friends. This put most of Wynnton at risk.

That night, I came home early. I brought the telephone for Dee. It wasn't the kind CJ wanted. That night we were able to talk. It wasn't much, but at least we broke the ice. We mostly talked about Dee. Why had she kept this to herself?

All night, Dee remained in my thoughts. The next morning, I felt she needed someone to comfort her. I told CJ to call her. Thoughts of her empty hospital bed kept coming to my mind. I was wondering if she was still alive. This was something I didn't share with CJ.

When CJ made the telephone call, there was no answer. That's when I suggested she go to check on her. She rejected my suggestion. I thought she was afraid Dee had passed. There was only one way we could know for sure. We needed to go to the house. I agreed to go with her to Dee's house. CJ tried to call her again. Dee's mother answered the telephone. She stated Dee had been taken to the hospital. She was on her way to the hospital. We told her we would come to the hospital later. My memory of the rest of the day is cloudy.

When I came home that night, CJ gave me the news. Dee had passed away. After learning this, I got really high. I mixed alcohol and illegal drugs. Inside I was hurting. CJ found me crying in the living room. Dee had died and we were all in this cycle together. One of my regular partners had a relationship with her. Did he know what she had? We had been shooting drugs together. This was troubling me deeply. There were a lot of us in this cycle; Ace, Herb, Lee, Betty, and the list went on. It stayed on my mind all night. The next day, I couldn't go stealing with the regular crew. I called someone different to ride with me. I needed enough money to allow me to take a few days off. We would need to purchase flowers and show our condolences.

One morning, I overheard CJ talking to Ma' Evelyn on the telephone. She wanted to view Dee's body. Still, she was afraid to go alone. She didn't ask me. For strength she chose to confide in her mother. She left the house and went to pick her mother up. She returned a short while later. She told me how good Dee looked. Afterwards, CJ and I went to the funeral home. Betty went with us. Dee looked extremely good. There was no sign of distress on her face.

The funeral was Saturday afternoon. I rode to the funeral with another friend. Memories flooded my mind. The church was familiar to me. In my younger days, I had played baseball for this church. This day, I was coming here for a different reason. It was time to pay my last respects to a dear friend. The funeral was packed. A lady spoke at the funeral. She spoke about repentance. She also shared Dee's last words. She told about Dee's vision of visiting her grandmother. Her grandmother had been dead a long time. Dee's suffering was over. She had broken the cycles. I spent the rest of the day medicating.

The next day was a Sunday. I was waiting in bed for the stores to open. Soon my monkey would be kicking. I was amazed to see CJ was already up. Lying there, I watched her getting ready. I wondered what was on her mind. I taught her to dress well when she went shopping. Today, she was dressed exceptionally well. She had on her fox coat. She didn't tell me where she was heading. I didn't ask. It was on my mind, but I didn't ask. I didn't know how she would respond. She left without a word to me. It started to bother me. We had been going at this for months. I decided to stay home.

Everlasting Love

Yea, I have loved thee with an everlasting love:
therefore in love and kindness have I drawn thee.
Jeremiah 31:3b

The voice offered no explanations, only this simple declaration, "It's over."

There was no need for an explanation; I understood the implications of this statement. This revelation wasn't based on a sermon, a song, or a prayer. This was a direct revelation from God at a time when I least expected it. The only thing on my mind was the pain I felt, the pain of losing Dee. There was also a lot of guilt. There were constant thoughts of things that should have been said to her. Was there a reason Dee hadn't shared her illness with me? Had I done something to offend her or that caused her to feel I would reject her? These things were plaguing my mind. I wasn't planning to hear from heaven about my salvation. This wasn't what I was looking for. I just wanted the pain and the guilt to subside. Unbeknown to me, God had other plans. My salvation was on His mind.

Can a maid forget her ornament, or a bride
her attire? Yet My people have forgotten Me
days without number. Jeremiah 2:32

"God I rejected you. I've tried to hide from your presence."

Like the father of the prodigal son, God had been waiting on me to come home. His arms were open wide, waiting to embrace me, waiting to welcome me back home. He was preparing a feast in my honor. He was giving me the best gift, the gift of eternal life.

> *Seek ye the Lord while He may be found, call ye upon Him while He is near: Let the wicked forsake his way, and the unrighteous man his thoughts: and let him return unto the Lord, and He will have mercy upon him; and to our God, for He will abundantly pardon. For My thoughts are not your thoughts, neither are your ways My ways, saith the Lord.*
> Isaiah 55:6-8

The God who is the God over time must have caused time to stand still. It took less than two minutes to walk to reach the front door of the church, but so much happened within this time. When He spoke these words, "It's over," I understood His words. I had run out of grace. I understood I had exhausted the patience of God. I understood before me had been placed a choice between life and death. There was a choice to be made between evil and good. Not only did I understand the choices, I understood the consequences. In the choices, there was actually only one choice. God was allowing me to choose my own fate. The answer was as clear as this scripture:

> *I call heaven and earth to record this day against you, that I have set before you life and death, blessing and cursing: therefore choose life, that both you and your seed may live.* Deuteronomy 30:7

Additionally, God revealed to me how He had intervened on my behalf on numerous occasions. It wasn't because I was good at stealing or good at selling drugs that I had survived on the street. It wasn't because I was smart that I hadn't been sent back to jail or prison. It wasn't because I was careful that He had spared me from AIDS. It wasn't because I was strong that He had spared me from drug addition. I had taken every step to become hooked! It wasn't because I was lucky that my life had been spared numerous times. My life had been in danger more times than I could have ever imagined. God revealed to me all the times that He had intervened to spare my life. It was because of His grace I had been spared. God knew the plans He had for my life. I didn't.

> For I know the thoughts that I think towards
> you, saith the Lord, thoughts of peace, and
> not of evil, to give you an expected end.
> Jeremiah 29:11

In my failure to acknowledge Him, somehow I thought I had left Him behind. At this time, He was revealing to me that in every wretched thing I had done, He was there, sparing me from the consequences of my actions. He was letting me know He would no longer interfere in my life, if this was what I really wanted. The choice was mine to make. He was ready to withdraw His hand of protection from me, if I wasn't ready to accept His intervention in my life, willingly. He had grown tired of my refusals to accept Him.

> For innumerable evils have compassed me
> about: mine iniquities have taken hold upon
> me, so that I am not able to look up; they are
> more than the hairs on mine head: therefore
> my heart faileth me. Be pleased, O Lord, to
> deliver me: O Lord, make haste to help me.
> Psalm 40:12-13

Growing clearer to me was the damage caused by my behavior. In my mind, I was the only person who was being harmed by my behavior. My children always had their material needs met. They never saw me getting high.

No one had been allowed to disrespect or abuse them. My mother had never seen me selling drugs or working the streets. It had never occurred to me to curse her out or beat her. Even in selling drugs, I had never introduced anybody to drugs. It was their choice. The people I sold drugs to were already hooked. Even in my stealing, the stores were already over charging for the merchandise. They had insurance on the goods. The insurance companies were ripping people off, too. After all the rich were getting richer at the expense of the poor and the poor were getting poorer. This wasn't fair. My actions were just helping to make things equal. This is what I was convinced of, until the scales fell from my eyes.

For the first time, I knew I hadn't been a good mother. My children had suffered tremendous shame and embarrassment because of my activities. My children didn't want things. They wanted me! They wanted to spend quality time with me. Additionally, there were other children being hurt. My selling drugs was helping to perpetuate the cycle of substance abuse. Drug addiction in those I loved had caused me terrible pain. Yet, I had contributed to this same pain in others. Then there was my mother. This was the revelation that was almost too painful to bear.

My mother had never given up on me, even when there was no reason to believe I would ever change. Inwardly bearing her pain, she had shown no outward signs of shame or embarrassment. My conduct was constantly thrown in her face. She had stood faithfully by me during my darkest days. She had kept my children when I was running the streets, providing a safe haven for them. When I attempted to pay her, she had refused to take anything from my ill-gotten gain. This had deeply offended me. She had held on when there were no signs I had any desire to change. How could I ever repay her for the humiliation and pain I had put her through?

Time had to be standing still because all of this was revealed unto me prior to my reaching the front door of the church. There was only a short distance from the parking lot to the front of the church and inside the church. The church foyer was small. My decision had already been made before entering the doors of the church. If God would still have me, I was willing to surrender to His will. My will was causing me too many problems. There was no need for an inward debate with myself.

My brother and sisters, if anyone among you wonder away from the truth and is brought back again, you can be sure that the one who brings that person back will save that sinner from death and bring about the forgiveness of many sins. James 5:19 (NLT)

Dee had died at an early age, but this wasn't a wasted death. Her death had served as the final catalyst turning my life around. I was coming home for good. I was unable to make it on my own and I was tired of trying. My life was out of control and I needed help. Mama wasn't surprised to see the prodigal daughter coming home. I was glad the doors were still open.

The LORD said, "If as one people speaking the same language they have begun to do this, then nothing they plan to do will be impossible for them. Genesis 11:6

My life would never be the same again. When I returned home, there were a couple things I needed to correct. The first thing I wanted to do was assure that there were no drugs left in the house. After searching the house thoroughly, all the drugs were flushed down the toilet. Then all of my cigarette papers were located and disposed of, tearing them to pieces, making sure they would be no good to any one who happened to find them. There were several bottles of wine in the dining room cabinet. Each one of these was opened and the wine poured into the sink. After this was finished, I turned to my biggest challenge, trying to rectify the problems in my marriage.

This was well after time for the stores to open. Sunday was a short workday. Normally, Buck would have been gone. His addiction wouldn't allow him to go for more than a few hours without his body going through withdrawals. The withdrawals weren't easy and they weren't pretty. Today, he was still in the bedroom waiting for me to return. The look I gave him was totally different from the one he had been given a few hours earlier. Tearfully, I apologized for trying to hurt him deliberately. He had done many things causing me pain, but they weren't done deliberately. Everything I had done for several months had been designed to hurt him and I had almost destroyed myself in the process. The next time I went to church, he went with me.

> Howbeit when He, the Spirit of truth is come,
> He will guide you into all truth: for He shall
> not speak of Himself; but whatsoever He
> shall hear, that shall He speak: and He shall
> show you things to come. John 16:13

God was working fast and He was restoring everything I had allowed the devil to steal from me. We were broke, but it didn't matter. We had something we had never had before...peace. There were still challenges within our relationship needing to be worked out.

Everlasting Love: The Flip Side

Thou knowest my downsitting and my uprising, Thou understandeth my thoughts afar off. Thou compassest my path and my lying down, and art acquainted with all my ways. For there is not a word in my tongue, but, lo, O Lord, thou knoweth it altogether. Thou hast beset me behind and before, and laid Thine hand upon me. Such knowledge is too wonderful for me; it is high, I cannot attain unto it. Whether shall I flee from thy presence? If I ascend up into heaven, thou art there: if I make my bed in hell, behold, thou art there. If I take the wings of the morning, and dwell in the uttermost parts of the sea; Even there thy hand shall lead me, and thy right hand shall hold me. Psalm 139:2-10

After CJ left the house, I went back to sleep. My sleep was interrupted by my thoughts. My monkey was waking up. There was a lot to think about. If I went to sleep too deeply, I would be in trouble. I needed to be alert to the changes in my body. Thoughts of my marriage were also troubling me. That's if it could be called a marriage. I was also wondering where she had gone. It would have been easier to ask before she left. We just weren't on those terms. In between my thoughts, I was dozing off to sleep.

When CJ returned home, I was still in bed. I heard her when she walked in the front door. She stopped in the kitchen. She was doing something at the kitchen sink. It sounded as if she was washing dishes. I could hear doors opening and closing. When she finished her tasks, I heard her walking down the hall.

CJ walked into our bedroom. I was looking up at her. There was something different about her. She didn't look angry. She took a seat on the bed near me. She began to explain where she had been. This somewhat surprised me. It was a good surprise. I was glad she had gone to church. This was a part of her past. It was a part of who she was. I knew she was a backslider. Traces of her relationship with God had remained.

"God has changed my life again. Buck, forgive me for the things I have said against you."

She reached out to me. Later, she climbed into bed next to me. She held me through the sickness. It took several days for me to completely kick the drugs. CJ remained by my side. Finally, there was hope for the marriage.

If the marriage was going to be salvaged, we needed God's help. He was our only hope. I decided to go to church with her. We needed to be on one accord. I didn't want the drugs to control the rest of my life.

We started attending church regularly. Stealing and drugging came to end. The temptation was always present. It seemed opportunities to take something were everywhere. There were traps everywhere. We ran from them.

After my strength returned, I began looking for employment. I found a job I liked. CJ was spending most of her time reading the Bible. She was growing. I had a different wife, a better wife. There were also the first HIV tests.

Unfinished Business

Redeeming the times because the days are evil.
Ephesians 5:16

Buck was working, legally working, and he loved his job. He was actively involved in the church. About six months after having confessed he had accepted Jesus Christ as his Lord and Savior, he was appointed a deacon. The missions looking for something to steal had ceased. His withdrawal from the heroin had gone smoothly and without any complications. Buck was no longer hiding. It appeared nobody was looking for him. Whenever we saw detectives who knew Buck well, he would have conversations with them. Either God had blocked the remembrance of the warrant for his arrest from their minds, or Buck's appearance was remarkably different, since his system was clean from all the drugs.

Buck began to push me towards doing something constructive with my life. In doing this, he had no idea he was opening up an old wound. It was also a deep wound. These conversations were familiar to me. I remembered the old conversations with my grandfather like they were yesterday and my response was as if this was yesterday. He really wasn't concerned about whether I went to school or went to work. His desire was for me to do something positive with my life. This was viewed as his trying to shirk his responsibility for taking care of his family. I was spending hours reading the Bible each day. My response to him came directly from the Word.

But if any provide not for his own, and specially for those of his own house, he hath denied the faith, and is worse than an infidel.
1 Timothy 5:8

I wasn't ready to secure employment or education. Physically and emotionally, I still needed a lot of work and healing. My self-esteem had really been shattered by all the negative words spoken over my life. For years, I had been wearing long sleeves and turtlenecks or dickeys. This had nothing to do with the weather. When the weather was hot, I continued wearing excessive clothes.

Because Thy lovingkindness is better than life, my lips shall praise Thee. Psalm 63:3

While I liked nice furniture and my house clean, it was a real struggle for me to keep it clean. One day, when I was attempting to clean the house, God began to clean me. He began cleaning me from the root of my hurt. In a way only He can, He began to relate the struggle with the house with the struggle I was having within myself.

And He answered and spake unto those that stood before Him, saying. Take away the filthy garments from Him. And unto him He said, Behold, I have caused thine iniquity to pass from thee, and I will clothe thee with a change of raiment. Zechariah 3:4

The shame I felt when people stared at me caused me to feel like a freak. Conscience people were staring at me; the pain had been internalized. Additionally, I lived in fear someone would find out about my checkered past and reject me. The secrets I was trying to hide made me feel dirty, used, abused, rejected, and neglected. It was too much to risk being hurt again. It was easier to remain trapped inside my comfort zone, hiding behind my clothes, hoping no one would ever discover my dirty secrets. If it was left up to me, I was going to take my secrets, my pain, and my silent tears to my grave. There was safety inside my comfort zone.

God began to explain to me how good He had been to me in the midst of my worst trials. The glory of God had been revealed in His delivering me each time I had been counted out. As for the turtlenecks and long sleeves, this was my shield and defense against the world. They said, "don't ask me what happened to me; the subject is off limits."

For years, whenever someone had asked me about the burns my choice was to ignore the question or change the subject. Whenever the burns were discussed, I was selective in what was told.

God said, "Tell the whole story. This is a way for you to glorify Me. In the midst of the fire, I was with you. In the midst of your recovery, I was with you. Whenever you tell it, tell the whole story."

By hiding behind my clothes, I was missing the opportunity to witness for Him. The dickeys were coming off! No longer would I wear long sleeves, as a necessity, each day. It took most of the day for me to clean the house. In the aftermath, walls had been washed, floors mopped, brass polished and crystal cleaned, all with my tears. My physical house and my spiritual house were cleaner than they had ever been. When the opportunity presented itself, I would be able to relate the whole story.

This was only the beginning. Now God was taking away the shame, I was moving towards fulfilling His purpose in my life. He was expecting more from me! This was a small morsel for my journey, but for now, this was enough. God was feeding me slowly.

And I thank Christ Jesus our Lord, who hath enabled me, for that He counted me faithful, putting me into the ministry; Who was before a blasphemer, and persecutor, and injurious: but I obtained mercy... 1 Timothy 1:12-13

I knew God wanted me to do something, but I didn't know what. My mother and I been faithfully ministering at the county jail for more than a year. She had become my best friend and companion in the ministry. I was willing to share my experiences in the street, during these Sunday visits, if this would help someone else. However, God wanted more from me. But what?

But he that knew not, and did commit things worthy of stripes, shall be beaten with few stripes. For unto whomsoever much is given, of him shall be much required: and of whom men have committed much, of him they will ask the more. Luke 12:48

My daughter had wanted to be a lawyer since she was two years old. At this time, she was in the twelfth grade. She thought the dream was out of her reach. Desperately, I wanted her to fulfill her goals. My life had been a failure, but I wanted more for her. All of my expectations for a better future were wrapped up in Earline. Somehow, I think she was watching my example rather than listening to what was said. I had given up doing anything professionally with my life. My life would be spent trying to repair the damage caused by my past. My contributions to society would center on my ministry.

However, the more I began to push Earline, God began to impress upon my heart I could do more. I had no idea what this could be.

By this time, the inmates at the Muscogee County jail knew me better than most people did. I decided to ask them what I could do to make a difference in the world, since I had no idea. There was almost unanimous agreement, based on my history, I would make a good AIDS or drug counselor. These choices seemed like good possibilities and careers, which might interest me. Hence, there was a willingness to pursue these choices.

> *Now our Lord Jesus Christ himself, and God, even our Father, which hath loved us, and hath given us everlasting consolation and good hope through grace, Comfort your hearts, and establish you in every good word and work.* 2 Thessalonians 3:13

There was no understanding on my part of what it would take for me to become a counselor. In the beginning, the thought of having to attend college for four years was upsetting to me. Now that my mind was made up to go back to work, my desire was to do this quickly. So much of my life had been wasted frivolously, I didn't want to waste anymore time. I was ready to discontinue the public assistance, which had been my crutch for a number of years. God was at work on my behalf. Because of limited knowledge, I just didn't understand this. My prayer had already become "God help me to accept your will, even when I don't understand."

It had been over a year since Buck had been free from active drug addiction. However, his appearance or behavior on drugs had never been forgotten. He began reading the Bible less, not that he had ever been an avid Bible reader. Sometimes, he wouldn't come directly home from work. He began spending more time at his mother's house and with some of his family members who were obviously not living for Jesus. His mother's house was part of his addiction playground. My suspicion was aroused. I suspected he was dabbling with drugs again. However, when I checked his body for fresh needle marks, none could be found anywhere. A new cycle was getting ready to begin.

One night after I left church, I decided to go by Buck's job. This was well after time for him to be off. His car was there, but Buck had been gone for hours. Knowing my suspicions were right about him, I decided to teach another person to drive. This was Earline's first driving lesson. Removing the key from my key ring, I placed it into the ignition and cranked the car. It was explained to Earline there was no need to be afraid. Crystal had been taught how to drive using this same method. She was given the same instructions, which had been provided Crystal years earlier.

"This is the brake and this is the gas. When you see my brake light come on put your foot on the brake. This is the signal. When I put my signal on, you put yours on. Trust me and stay close to me. Don't be afraid. This is the way I taught Crystal to drive a car."

We took almost the exact route, which had been taken with Crystal years earlier. From the rearview mirror, I observed her driving and she was doing fine. She stayed close to me. Driving very carefully, we made it to the house. Earline told me she cried all the way home. I had prayed all the way home.

That night, Buck didn't come home and I began packing his clothes. If there was anything I was convinced of, it was there was no room in my life for this mess. I didn't want the spirits attached with the streets living in the house with me. The first hand knowledge I received about letting those demons who had been evicted move back in was still in the forefront of my mind. When Buck returned home, he was served his eviction notice. This was nothing new to him. There was no need for explanations. This was the cycle: abuse of drugs, eviction, conviction, apology, honeymoon, abuse of drugs, and so the cycle went.

A few days after he left, I became concerned about him. While convinced he was abusing illegal drugs, something just didn't add up. He continued going to work and coming to church. Buck's heroin habit averaged between $300 and $500 a day. There was no way a job could be supplying him adequate money for this type of habit. Furthermore, the teaching I was hearing convicted me about my actions. My decision was made to let him come back home. This started a pattern of me putting him out, being convicted for my actions, and telling him to come home. Finally, it was apparent what was going on with him. He had changed drugs. He was using crack.

Wives, submit yourselves unto your own husbands, as unto the Lord. For the husband is the head of the wife, even as Christ is the head of the church: and He is the Savior of the body. Therefore as the church is subject unto Christ, so let the wives be to their own husbands in everything. Husbands, love your wives, even as Christ also loved the church, and gave Himself for it, that He might sanctify and cleanse it with the washing of water by the word, that He might present it to Himself a glorious church, not having spot, or wrinkle, or any such thing, but that it should be without blemish. So ought men to love their wives as their own bodies. He that loveth his wife loveth himself. For no man ever yet hated his own flesh; but nourisheth and cherisheth it, even as the Lord the church. For we are members of His body, of His flesh, and of His bones. For this cause shall a man leave his father and mother. And shall be joined unto his wife, and they two shall be one flesh. This is a great mystery: but I speak concerning Christ and the church. Ephesians 5:22-32

Paul was writing about the type of relationship a husband and wife should have with each other. He wrote that wives should submit themselves to their husbands in all things. He further explains the husbands should love their wives as Christ loved the church, even sacrificing himself for it. I reasoned if Buck loved me as Christ loved the church, I would have no problem submitting to him. Since he didn't love me like this, there was no reason for me to submit to him. I didn't tell him, but whenever he gave me a choice or failed to give me clear guidelines, I did it Charlotte's way. Whenever, he gave me a clear directive, I compiled with his request because I was mindful of this scripture. There was one problem; Buck's normal way of communicating with me always allowed me a way of escape. Normally, I took the way of escape.

Here's an example of my manipulative behavior. Buck had started using drugs again. The next step to follow was for me to put him out of the house. To be more exact, I couldn't put him out the house. However, I could put his clothes out and worry him to follow the clothes! During one of these periods, I celebrated my birthday. He was never prone to miss celebrating or acknowledging any special occasions. This one would be no different. He took me out to lunch, but I could tell he was very impatient. He was ready for the date to be over so he could get on with his daily activities. To be honest, the 'monkey' on his back was giving him a fit, the drug addiction. We had an argument and lunch ended abruptly. We were expecting a large check at the end of the week. Well, the check came that day. The next morning, I went on a shopping spree and spent the whole check. The day the check was supposed to arrive, Buck called me.

"CJ, did the check come today?"

"No Buck, it didn't come today."

A few days later, he came by the house. When he saw all the new furniture, he smiled and said, "I know my wife."

By this time, I was no longer angry and I was looking for a way to tell him I had spent the check. Relieved, I responded, "What do you know about your wife?"

"She loves to shop."

"And what else?"

He hadn't figured out what he needed to know about me. Whenever, I was upset, I went shopping. For over a month, he called every day and repeated his question

"CJ, did the check come today?"

"No Buck, it didn't come today."

Finally, he called and said, "CJ did the check come any day?"

"Yes, Buck."

"When did the check come?"

"On my birthday."

"What happened to the check?"

"I bought the furniture. I thought you had figured it out when you said you knew me."

From the beginning of our relationship, we had established a rule we would never go to bed angry with each other. We did not always adhere to the rule, but we were never prone to be angry with each other for an extended period of time. Most of the time, our differences were resolved before we went to bed. This time, he wanted to be angry with me, but that's not his nature. In a couple of days, he decided to come back home. He had actually forgiven me before I admitted what I had done. He knew I never wasted money. If I had blown the money recklessly, perhaps the outcome would have been different.

> *Thine own wickedness shall correct thee, and thy backslidings shall reprove thee: know therefore and see that it is an evil thing and bitter, that thou hast forsaken the LORD thy God, and that My fear is not in thee, saith the Lord GOD of hosts.* Jeremiah 2:19

It was about this time another tragedy occurred in our lives. Buck had been protected by God's grace for more than a year. However, he had chosen to walk from under the covering. The consequences of these actions were closing in on him. His nephew, Hatch, had been in jail for about six months on a traffic violation. The time had passed for him to be released, but he remained in jail, unable to be released. Unbeknown to us, when Hatch was arrested, rather than giving his on name, he had given Buck's name. He was confined indefinitely under Buck's charges. With mixed emotions, the can of worms had been packed away from view was opened.

The sheriff explained to me that he knew both Buck and Hatch well. He spoke to me over the telephone.

"I know who he is, but if he was stupid enough to use Buck's name, I'm not going to help him. Let him sit here."

Next, a call was placed to probation officer to appeal to him for help. He agreed at my request to go to the jail to compare their fingerprints. There was one problem when he went to make the comparison. Since Hatch had used Buck's name, all of the fingerprints under both names were coming up as belonging to Hatch. The probation officer didn't know how to correct the confusion.

With no other alternative, a telephone call I really dreaded was made. Calling the District Attorney's office was difficult and I almost decided to leave Hatch in jail. When the first call was made, I don't think they believed my explanation of how the mix-up occurred. Over a week had passed before someone was willing to review all the charges, which had ever been brought against each of them. Over the telephone, every attempt was made to help them distinguish who was the rightful owner of each charge. About a week after this, Buck's mother called to tell us Buck's name was in the newspaper. Hatch had been released and the whole story was printed in the newspaper. For the first time in almost two years, that night I couldn't sleep. My thoughts were on parole and police officers coming to my house. It was as if the fear had never left me.

> *For as many as are led by the Spirit of God, they are the sons of God. For ye have not received the spirit of bondage again to fear; but ye have received the Spirit of adoption, whereby we cry, Abba, Father. The Spirit itself beareth witness with our spirit, that we are the children of God.* Romans 8:14-16

When we paid the $10,000 to get Buck out jail on the possession charges, we had never planned on him going to court. The next day it was decided, Buck was going to turn himself in to face the charges. We met with our pastor to explain the circumstances. The pastor and most of the church agreed to support Buck through this process. Whenever Buck went to court on these charges, several members would take time off from work to provide support for him in the courtroom. The DA (district attorney) wasn't inclined to give Buck a break on the sentence for these charges. Buck's lawyer called my pastor and me outside the courtroom and told us what the DA was going to recommend to the judge. This sentence was unacceptable to both of us. The attorney didn't seem to care.

The attorney said, "Well, you can attempt to make a statement to the judge, but normally the judge sides with the recommendation of the DA. I don't think it will help."

We wanted the opportunity to speak. The judge agreed to hear us and each member of the church came forward to make a statement. After each of us had spoken, the judge rejected the DA's recommendation, cutting the recommended sentence in half. She sentenced Buck to three years. This was a miracle considering his record and was the lightest sentence he had ever received.

> *And whatsoever ye do, do it heartily, as to the Lord, and not unto men; Knowing that of the Lord ye shall receive the reward of the inheritance: for ye serve the Lord Christ.*
> Colossians 3:23-24

While Buck was locked up, I enrolled in college. God blessed me academically. Physically, God also blessed me. The campus was very hilly and attending classes on the campus would require me to do more walking than I had done since I had learned to walk again. The parking lots were a great distance from the classrooms. Before I started this college, I was unable to walk more than a block on a regular basis without becoming exhausted. My strength increased and I was able to make the daily tracks across campus without major complications. I only missed one day of school during my time at Columbus College. This day, I took my daughter to the University of Georgia for orientation.

Each Saturday, I visited Buck at the prison. I took my textbooks and notebooks with me. Most of our visit, he watched as I completed my homework. At other times, I used him to test the new skills I was learning. He wanted more of my attention. I asked him to be patient until I graduated. After all, he was the person who had insisted I do something with my life. During my last year of college, Buck was released from prison.

My soul shall make her boast in the Lord: the humble shall hear thereof, and be glad. O magnify the Lord with me, and let us exalt His name together. I sought the Lord, and He heard me, and delivered me from all my fears. Psalm 34:2-4

Before my graduation from Columbus College, I was selected to be a member of Phi Kappa Phi Honor Society. In addition, I received the Bachelor of Science Honors Award. After three years at Columbus College, I graduated magna cum laude with a 3.64 grade point average on a 4.0 scale. Evelyn Russell's daughter had finally done something positive! My husband, my mother, my children, and my academic advisor, Ms. Titus were at my graduation to support me. The people I thought would support me when I began doing something positive with my life weren't there. God sent others in their place!

During the time I had been attending college, I reported my progress to Buck's parole officer. The best graduation present I received was a recommendation to the Governor of Georgia that I be granted a full and complete pardon. Christmas 1994, I received the biggest Christmas present I had ever received, a full and complete pardon from the governor of Georgia!

In everything give thanks; for this is the will of
God in Christ Jesus concerning you.
1 Thessalonians 5:18

After all the struggles and trials in my life, it seemed to me there would be a chorus of family and friends at each milestone, shouting, "Thank God! She finally did something right." This wasn't to be. With the exception of a few people, who invested in the promise, God was the source of my strength and my refuge. My tears asked, "God why?" Moreover, it seemed to me, in the distance, I heard a chorus of Black Sheep shouting; "We made it over."

Unfinished Business: The Flip Side

God is our refuge and strength, a very present help in trouble. Therefore will not we fear, though the earth be removed, and though the mountains be carried into the midst of the sea; though the waters thereof roar and be troubled, though the mountains shake with the swelling thereof. Psalm 46:1-3

Things went well for several months. That is, until I got comfortable. On the surface, it appeared we were a normal family. My drug addiction was a thing of the past. I was no longer hiding from the parole officers. Financially we were starting to get ahead legally.

Foolishly I started experimenting with drugs again. When I reverted back to my old behavior, she pulled one of hers out. She demanded I leave the house. I moved in with one of my nephews. I continued going to church. No one was aware of the separation. As time passed, it was becoming harder to keep up the pretense.

Eventually, CJ had a moment of remorse and came looking for me. It was an ugly confrontation. I felt pressured to lie to her again. If I told her the truth, it might end the marriage. I lied. That night, I moved back home. I tried to kick the habit again and get our lives back on track. There was something that made this harder. I had traded drugs. Crack wouldn't turn loose easily. I thought this drug would be easier to hide from her. It didn't take much for her to become suspicious. She was searching my body for the evidence. She also insisted on another HIV test. This started a new cycle in our life. She would get upset and ask me to leave home. Afterwards, she would be convicted and apologize. We went around this cycle for several months. It was interrupted by circumstances out of our control.

We got a call; my nephew was in jail. After several months he was still locked up with no sign of release. My mother asked CJ to look into it. What she discovered opened up a nightmare. He was locked up under my name. When she told me this I was sick. The mix-up needed to be cleared up. This meant drawing attention to unfinished business. The charges were still waiting on me. Freeing my nephew meant drawing heat on me. It was a hard choice. He had already served six extra months. I was enjoying my freedom.

Eventually, CJ was able to get the charges cleared up. Hatch was released. This meant trouble for me. The day after his release, my mother called with the news.

"You need to go get a newspaper."

When we read the newspaper, there it was. My full name was in the newspaper. The whole mix-up with Hatch was spelled out. It was an unwanted interruption. We knew this might happen. We weren't prepared for it to happen so soon. It was the wrong time. For months, I had been trying to get CJ to do something with her life. She was just coming around.

It was time to finish the business that had been lingering. Preparations had to be made for my surrender. We went to see the lawyer we had paid years earlier. After this meeting, we met with our pastor.

The next morning accompanied by my pastor and my wife, I went to the parole office. We had called my parole officer to let him know I was going to turn myself in. As we were waiting in the lobby, the other parole officer passed by and called me John Henry. As usual, I ignored him.

My parole officer came out to get us. As he completed the paperwork, we talked at length in his office. When the paperwork was completed, they left. At this point, I was handcuffed and taken to the jail. I had escaped from prison more than once, been on the run more than once, nevertheless, here I was giving myself up.

But then God our Savior showed us His kindness and love. He saved us not because of the good things we did, but because of His mercy. He washed away all of our sins and gave us a new life through the Holy Spirit. He generously poured out the Spirit upon us because of what Jesus Christ our Savior did. He declared us not guilty because of His great kindness. Titus 3:4-7a (NLT)

CJ continued to work for me on the outside. She reported everything going on to our pastor. When I went to court, the church was there for me. The case was put off several times. Several members continued to come to the courtroom. The DA offered me a plea bargain. My lawyer thought I should take it. It was too much time for the amount of money we had paid him. In the end, I didn't know what was going to happen.

And the LORD said, "I will cause all my goodness to pass in front of you, and I will proclaim my name, the LORD, in your presence. I will have mercy on whom I will have mercy, and I will have compassion on whom I will have compassion. Exodus 33:19

The lawyer met with CJ and our pastor before court began. I pleaded guilty, but there was an additional request. Several people from the church wanted to address the court on my behalf. I had been before this judge before. She allowed them to speak. In the end, she showed me mercy. I received the lightest sentence I had ever been given.

After several months, I was shipped to a county camp. Some members of the church came to see me there. The chaplain at the camp took an active interest in the inmates. He did everything he could to motivate us. He went beyond his official duties. He even visited my church in Columbus several times. I was actively involved in the spiritual activities at the prison. One of the ministers from our church came down to minister at the chapel. CJ and my sister came with him.

CJ was enrolled in college. Each time, she came to see me, she brought homework with her. At one point in her education, she conducted a survey on the inmates. She was focused on her education.

I was released before she graduated from college. She had resisted my pushing her. However, my efforts were paying off.

Lord let it be my Way

For I hate divorce!" says the LORD, the God of Israel. "It is as cruel as putting on a victim's bloodstained coat," says the LORD Almighty. "So guard yourself; always remain loyal to your wife." Malachi 2:16 (NLT)

When Buck began abusing crack, it started another cycle in our lives. I had been desperate to marry him. Now, I was desperate to divorce him. The heroin addiction offered some hope. I knew heroin had a bottom out cycle (a point a user would no longer desire the drug). An addict would reach this point, if they lived long enough. Crack was different. The drug causes rapid aging and deterioration of the body. I also knew it as a drug for petty criminals. The smell of the drug is horrible. The smell of it was sickening to me. If an addict removes his shoes within 30 feet of you, it can make you pass out. This drug addict has no family or loved ones. All they care about is feeding their habit. They will abuse or use anyone to achieve this purpose. It is a fast agent, causing rapid and mass destruction. It is a drug I wanted no part of directly or indirectly.

I don't know what possessed Buck to try it. He had seen the effects of the drug. There was no room in his life for me. Buck had his own holes needing to be filled. He kept looking for answers in the drugs. This ultimately kept him revolving in and out of prison. While he was in prison, I had to be the head of the house. I was determined to be good at it and I became comfortable in the role. Whenever

Buck returned home, I wanted him to assume the role of the head of the house. Still, I didn't know how to turn loose or step aside. My way was the right way and I kept worrying him to get it right. This kept confusion in our family and kept the cycle going. We were two halves who had joined together to make a quarter. Some people say two halves make a whole, not in a marriage.

There were too many complications. We were trying to be something we didn't have a clue about how to become. There was a lot of growing that needed to be done in both of our lives. He didn't know how to love me and I didn't know how to receive what he was trying to give me, his version of love. His love for the drugs kept me feeling insecure for years. I just couldn't compete with them. Finally, I decided to stop trying. We were both miserable. It seemed pointless to keep the relationship up. I wanted a husband, but that's not what I was getting.

Outside interference was always controlling our relationship. It was always what "somebody else wanted." It was "something somebody said." It was "something somebody needed." In his efforts to please other people, he risked destroying himself. He risked destroying me. Ultimately, it destroyed our relationship.

For years, the trap was obvious. Each time, it started with pressure outside of our relationship. In some ways he was so strong. Still, when it came to saying no to some people, it wasn't his nature. They pulled in one direction and I pulled in another. Each time, they won. He yielded to the pressure, returning to his favorite playground. The trigger was squeezed and there it was again. The cycle was continuing to spiral out of control.

As he returned to his first love, I begged God to let me divorce him. He couldn't stay in the house with me. I had left this lifestyle behind. I valued my freedom and serenity. Each time, I forced him to leave our home, I felt God intervening for him. Each time, I decided to end the relationship, there would be some teaching on marriage or forgiveness convicting me. Off I would go to find him. After apologizing, I promised to stand by him through his recovery. In a few days, he would go back to the drugs. I couldn't deal with it and the cycle repeated. It repeated for years and I kept begging God for my freedom.

In the beginning, I was begging Buck to stop abusing drugs. Then, I began begging God to deliver him.

At this juncture, I was no longer asking Him to deliver Buck, I was begging for permission to end the marriage. The last time I asked God about divorcing him, there was no answer. God was silent. I took this as permission to do it my way. When I decided to end the marriage, the love was still there. I loved Buck and I knew he loved me. Love just wasn't enough. We needed something stronger than love, if the marriage was going to survive. It seemed to me that we didn't have what it was going to take for the survival of our relationship. I remembered the vision God had given me of Buck in the pulpit, but I wanted to forget it.

He wasn't being consistent in His walk with God. Enough was enough! There were too many issues. Too many holes needed to be filled. There was too much pain in the relationship for it to be salvaged. His drug usage had caused me a lot of pain. I had been faithful in responding to his drug usage with razor sharp words that pierced his heart. With my salvation, my words had taken on a new twist. I knew how to divide the scriptures to suit my needs. I kept condemning him with my words. I was too impatient and hurting too bad to wait for The Word to bring conviction. For years, I didn't understand the difference between condemnation and conviction.

There were many confrontations, which got out of hand. It was part of the cycle. On more than one occasion, I looked for Buck. Normally, I found him. In the early years of our relationship, he came home with me easily. Even when I wasn't looking for him, I ran into him. It happened on any street or any side of town. It even happened in different cities.

Over the years, there was more than one high-speed chase. My niece (his niece by blood, mine by choice) often accompanied me on these trips. There was the time she ran his car off the road. She was driving my car. There was the time we chased him through Wynnton. His car needed major repairs. He was trying to get away, but the car left a thick trail of smoke around each corner.

As the years passed, I looked for him less. However, periodically, the cycle flared up again. My niece liked to help me find him. He wasn't living at home. His mother called and asked me to find him. She was worried. The best place to start was at my niece's apartment.

"Auntie, I haven't seen him, but I'm tired of him worrying Mama. It's been a long time since I have had some excitement. Wait and I'll go with you."

This was the night the chase went through Wynnton and two adjoining subdivisions. My niece was hanging out the window, shooting at the car. Actually, she wasn't trying to hit the car. She was trying to scare them. Buck's car almost cut off several times. In the end, he left the car parked in the middle of the road, with the keys in the ignition. The car was still running. It was the last time he saw the car. It was one of the last times I went looking for him.

Frustrated, I walked away from the man I loved. I decided to let God have him because I just couldn't handle him any more. Buck prayed for God to intervene. He learned how to pray for his wife. There had to be a way to repair the damage. When I told him I had filed the papers for the divorce, I don't think he believed me. He tried to talk to me, but my mind was made up. Knowing he would not sign the divorce papers, I filed for divorce by publication. I said I didn't know where he was located. In actuality, I knew how to find him. I didn't know where he was at that exact moment.

The day I went for the hearing, I couldn't get the facts straight in my head. I couldn't remember the year we were married. I couldn't remember how long we had been separated. There had been so many separations. There was a sense of uneasiness about what I was doing. The choice was made to ignore it. I had also petitioned for my name to be changed. With a flick of the pen, I effectively ended the years of turmoil. If only it were that simple.

Throughout the marriage, I had been Charlotte Russell Johnson. With the divorce, my name was Charlotte Russell again. When I walked out of the courtroom, I didn't feel like Ms. Russell. She was my mother. Sister Russell was my mother. I didn't feel like Charlotte Russell Johnson. It was the first time I had felt like Charlotte Johnson. This troubled me.

When I received the final decree, I mailed him a copy of it. Eventually, I went to see him. We were still friends. He was still shocked by what I had done. We talked a few times, but there was no reconciliation. After a few months, we talked again. We developed a nasty pattern of communication. It was hard for us to relate to

228

each other as two single people. Whenever one of us crossed the boundary, the other responded.

"You know, I'm not married to you," Buck would say.

It didn't feel right when he said this to me. In fact, I resented it every time he said it. Actually, it hurt. After this had gone on for a couple of months, I couldn't take any more.

"How do you feel when I tell you that?"

Buck responded, "I don't like it!"

"Well, why do you keep saying it to me?"

And if a woman shall put away her husband, and be married to another, she committeth adultery. Mark 10:12

We had no answers. We didn't like being divorced, but we couldn't live with each other. Buck kept the divorce a secret and continued wearing his ring. I gave my wedding band to Herman. For almost two-years after the divorce, I felt tied to him. We didn't talk regularly or see each other, but the bond remained. We were at a standstill. Where would the relationship go from here? Nothing about our relationship had ever been simple.

Since I still felt in my heart I was his wife. I threw the choice to him. Buck told me he wanted to date me for two-years before we remarried. He planned out the courtship. The two-years would begin upon his release. This was a trap. I wasn't going to play with the relationship. I told him to call me in two-years. If I was still free, we would look at our relationship. After all, I believed his words had freed me from our relationship.

It was about this time I told God something. It seemed like a perfect plan.

"God for the next two-years, I'm not going to be involved in any relationship. I don't want to be hurt and I don't want to be taken advantage of. In two-years, I'll start dating and get married again."

This seemed to be a good thing. Any thoughts of Buck were put out of my mind. Most of my life, I had been committed to someone. For the first time in years, I was free. There was no one to answer to. There were no arguments, no heartache. There were no late night meals to be prepared. In fact, I almost stopped cooking completely.

In two years, I was going to meet someone. This went on for more than a year. I was content with my vow. I began to meet different single people who seemed almost desperate to get married. I couldn't understand it. Being single was wonderful. However, I knew I didn't have the gift of singleness. One day I would remarry. I wasn't dating. I wasn't looking for a date. Nevertheless, I was enjoying being free of the hassles that come with marriage.

Everything was going fine. My time was totally committed to God and my ministry. He was my priority. Nothing else mattered to me except pleasing Him. My life had been totally submitted to Him. At least, I thought so. He ordered every one of my steps. For the first time in my life He was truly Lord of my life. I had come face to face with this choice. I had chosen Him. Everything in my life had been sacrificed to please Him. In the end, I had lost nothing. He had been faithful in providing for me. Things were going well. At least, I thought so. That is until God decided to show me something.

Whenever single women shared their stories with me, I had listened. I even wanted to show compassion. My flesh wasn't burning. In fact, if you didn't fan the coals, the fire wouldn't ignite. It was working for me. One by one, they came to me. I just couldn't figure it out. That is until

God gave me the mirror. When I looked into it I didn't like what I saw. Indeed, my thoughts had been judgmental. The vow I had made to Him had been made out of fear. I didn't want to be hurt. I didn't want to be taken advantage of. There had been enough pain in my life. I didn't want to risk being hurt again. Safety and security was what I wanted. I didn't want to take any risks. Before getting involved in another relationship, I wanted God to speak audibly and with clarity.

"This is it. He's the one for you. Marry him."

Shouldn't it be this simple? We tell God how to work, and He moves according to our specifications. Everything works out perfectly as we had planned it. It just doesn't work that way. Life is not so simple. God is too wise not to intervene for His children. We don't know what to ask for. Therefore, He helps us.

Then something shocking came to my attention. I had forgotten to ask God what He wanted me to do. When I made the two-year vow, it seemed like a good idea. Wouldn't God be pleased with me not dating? At least, it seemed this way to me. When I found out I was wrong it scared me. I wasn't prepared. My plan was not His plan. This sent me into a panic. What did He have in mind? I called for the saints to pray.

"Please pray I meet the right person. I don't want to be deceived."

Lord let it be my Way: The Flip Side

You cry out, "Why has the LORD abandoned us?" I'll tell you why! Because the LORD witnessed the vows you and your wife made to each other on your wedding day when you were young. But you have been disloyal to her, though she remained your faithful companion, the wife of your marriage vows. Didn't the LORD make you one with your wife? In body and spirit you are His.
Malachi 2:14-15a (NLT)

On the surface, everything seemed to be going well. I was working legally. Each day, I rode home from work with a friend from the job. On the way home each day, he had a regular stop. He stopped to get beer. It began with a beer. This was all it took to open the cycle. It wasn't long before CJ became suspicious. I tried to be careful. She couldn't prove a thing.

One day, I was in the midst of a transaction. that's when I ran into Crystal, CJ's sister. It was only a matter of time before my double life was going to be exposed. I wasn't looking forward to going home. She told CJ where she had seen me.

When I got home, CJ was waiting for me. She had searched the house and located some merchandise I had taken. She was in a rage. She was demanding I move out of the house.

You ask, "Why?" It is because the LORD is acting as the witness between you and the

wife of your youth, because you have broken
faith with her, though she is your partner, *the*
wife of your marriage covenant.
Malachi 2:14 (NIV)

The cycles kept repeating. There were times when I went on a binge and everything got out of control. There is one episode that still puzzles me. It had been several days since I had seen my mother. Since our breakup, I had been living with my mother. When I started using, I got into it with CJ. It was better for me to leave home. It was better for me to be somewhere that would allow me the freedom to indulge.

On this occasion, my mother called CJ. She asked her to find me. CJ agreed to find me for her. She enlisted the aide of my niece (her niece) to locate me. She acted more like she was CJ's niece. She was always in a conspiracy against me with CJ. Afterwards, she would offer one explanation for her actions.

"Uncle Buck, Auntie made me do it."

When CJ and my niece found me, they wanted to talk to me. I was trying to sell the merchandise we had taken. When I was located, there were two other people with me. Ace and his girlfriend were in my car. We had been working together. We were parked in Wynnton.

My niece walked up to the side of the car and told them to get out the car. Ace's girlfriend said something to her. I didn't hear what it was. My niece had a gun. She was acting crazy. I drove off. They followed behind me. It was a chase through the hood. My car wasn't running well. I couldn't shake them.

The integrity of the upright guides them,
but the unfaithful are destroyed by their
duplicity... Proverbs 11:3 (NIV)

We had a load of goods in the car. The best thing for me to do was to let them have the car. We took the merchandise from the car. I left the car and the keys. This would buy me some time. Our destination was nearby. I could see the car later. At least, that's what I thought. We split the merchandise up. I stayed out of sight; CJ might be still riding around the neighborhood.

Later that night, I saw my car parked on the corner of Annette Avenue and Buena Vista Road. However, I didn't have any keys with me. There was no sign of the driver. That was the last time I saw the car. I asked a policeman if the car had been towed.

"Yes! All the windows had been busted out"

I didn't bother going to the impound lot. The car needed major repairs. In my heart, I knew the car had been destroyed. It was a coward who destroyed my car. No one ever told me what happened. I kept inquiring, to no avail. To this day, no one has told me what happened to my car that night. I figured it was a woman's thing.

When you added it all up, crime really does pay. It was just the way it paid, which made it not worthwhile. It had dividends. They didn't always seem fair. Whenever I was hustling, I averaged about $500 a day profit. There were periods when it was more or less. There were times when I had a long run. There were other times when it only lasted a few months. Usually, by the time I was arrested, the money was gone. There were bond fees and lawyer fees needing to be paid. This was providing a bond was obtainable. Once locked up, I needed packages and money for personal items. Additionally, I needed letters and visitors. I also needed to make telephone calls, which were a financial burden. Sometimes a ten-minute collect call home cost $27. Even with all this, I kept going back to the cycle.

234

O LORD, though our iniquities testify against us, do Thou it for Thy name's sake: for our backslidings are many; we have sinned against Thee. Jeremiah 14:7

CJ had threatened to divorce me before. She never went through with it. The drugs told me this would be no different. It was on my mind. Most of the time when she told me something, it happened. Later, someone told me they had seen the divorce announcement in the paper. I knew it was serious. There was nothing I could do about it. The drugs were controlling my thoughts.

After I was busted, I had time to weigh my losses. Through prayer, reconciliation might be possible. Hopefully, she wouldn't become involved with anyone else before I was released. I knew it was unlikely she would commit to a relationship with anyone else. The person would have to be "saved." This gave me reason to remain hopeful. Also, weighing heavily on my mind were my crimes.

This bid was the cruelest extractor. It cost me five years of my life. I lost my wife and family. In the end, the thing I feared the most hit home.

God's Plan

*As for God, His way is perfect: the word of the LORD is
tried: He is a buckler to all those that trust in Him.*
Psalm 18:30

One day, as I was driving down the street, Buck crossed my mind. It was nothing special. It was just his name. For several days, I heard his name. I couldn't shake it. Maybe if I wrote him a letter, it would go away. I sent him the letter. It was probably more of a note. There were two sentences.

"Why didn't you answer my last letter? Who is Vanessa to you?"

It had been over a year since I sent the letter. Vanessa was nobody to him. I just didn't have anything else to say. He answered the letter by requesting to call me at an agreed upon time. When he called, I understood better why he had been in my spirit. His brother was terminally ill. He got the news around the same time that he got my note. There was no talk of love. It was an almost casual conversation between distant friends.

The next day, I felt a new message in my spirit.

"You need to go see him."

For two days, I shook the message off. It kept coming back. On the third day, I decided to write him. It was possible I might come for a visit. I forgot to write the letter. The next day, it came up again. On the way out the door, I grabbed a note pad. Before I drove five blocks from the house, I passed about five mail trucks. This got my attention. I needed to send the note. I pulled over to the side of the road. I wrote one sentence.

"If I'm not speaking Sunday, I'm coming to see you."

I stopped the mailman and handed him the note.

I told him, "this person must need this note."

Saturday night, I was driving back to Columbus. Buck's sister called me.

She told me, "Charlotte, Michael died this morning."

I responded, "I was planning to visit Buck tomorrow."

"I'd like to go with you."

When we arrived, I couldn't believe I was there. For almost five hours, I stared at him. There was very little said between us. What was there to say? As he talked with his sister, I watched him. I watched his pain. My heart was filled with compassion for him. It wasn't love I was feeling. In my heart, I knew God wanted me here with him. This was not in my plan. My plans were for a new relationship, with someone new. When we left him, my eyes were strained from staring at him.

I will heal their backsliding, I will love them
freely: for mine anger is turned away from
him. Hosea 14:4

God restored the relationship, but He gave me a new love for him. He gave me an appreciation for him I didn't have before. Part of this came as I was writing my second book, *Daddy's Hugs*. When I began to interview the children in our family, they told me things about him I had overlooked. Through my hurt and pain, I had been focussed on the negatives.

Charity suffereth long, and is kind; charity
envieth not; charity vaunteth not itself, is not
puffed up, Doth not behave itself unseemly,

seeketh not her own, is not easily provoked, thinketh no evil; Rejoiceth not in iniquity, but rejoiceth in the truth; Beareth all things, believeth all things, hopeth all things, endureth all things. Charity never faileth: but whether there be prophecies, they shall fail; whether there be tongues, they shall cease; whether there be knowledge, it shall vanish away. 1Corinthians 13:4-8

In recent months, I have come to realize Buck loves me unconditionally. That's important to me. After all, love is supposed to be unconditional. Even in marriage it's often hard to love this way. Moreover, yes, the love is reciprocal.

After the honeymoon, we are left with reality. Often times, it wasn't love. It was lust. What happens when the lust or passion is abated? How do you find unconditional love? How do you find a love that builds the other person up? Where do you find sacrificial love? Where do you find unselfish love? Where do you find love that forgives? Where do you find the love to commit until death do we part? Where do you find the love lasting through sickness and health? It's easier to love in health than it is in sickness, but what happens when one of the partners faces a major health crisis? What happens when outside influences constantly threaten to destroy the marriage relationship? What happens when one partner has difficulty forsaking all others? What happens when there is no cleaving? Where do you find unconditional love during the hard times? This kind of love is only possible when Christ is at the center of the marriage.

Who ever said marriage was easy? Who ever said it was supposed to be easy? Who created the myth? What happens when you don't walk off happily ever after into the sunset? What do you do on the days when you don't feel like being married? What happens when you can't agree and you don't want to agree? What happens when the answers aren't easy?

> *Nevertheless, to avoid fornication, let every man have his own wife, and let every woman have her own husband. Let the husband render unto the wife due benevolence: and likewise also the wife unto the husband. The wife hath not power of her own body, but the husband: and likewise also the husband hath not power of his own body, but the wife. Defraud ye not one the other, except it be with consent for a time, that ye may give yourselves to fasting and prayer; and come together again, that Satan tempt you not for your incontinency. But I speak this by permission, and not of commandment. For I would that all men were even as I myself. But every man hath his proper gift of God, one after this manner, and another after that. I say therefore to the unmarried and widows, It is good for them if they abide even as I. But if they cannot contain, let them marry: for it is better to marry than to burn.*
> 1Corinthians 7:2-16

Marriage is work. It's hard work. There are days when it's like chocolate covered cherries. In spite of its sweetness, there are days when it's more like a hot kosher pickle. There are days when I want to throw up my hands and walk away. There are other days when I say; "I can't do it." It's on those days I'm reminded He can. It's all about His plan and learning to put the marriage in His hands.

God's Plan: The Flip Side

Ever since the days of your ancestors, you have scorned
My laws and failed to obey them. Now return to Me, and I
will return to you, says the LORD Almighty. But you ask,
'How can we return when we have never gone away?'
Malachi 3:7 (NLT)

A strange thing happened during my last incarceration. My younger brother, Michael was sent to the prison where I was serving time. Normally, siblings weren't allowed to be incarcerated at the same facility. This had to be the mercy of God. It gave me time to mend my relationship with him. It also gave me time to witness to him. My actions on the outside of the prison were less than Christ like. However, I knew God was real. In prison I tried to live up to my profession of faith. I was actively involved in Bible study and worship services.

Mike's health began to decline rapidly. He went to the state hospital several times for tests. The last time he went for an operation. After four months, he wrote me a letter. The hospitalization was lasting longer than he had anticipated. They had operated. An infection had set in. He was in some discomfort. He asked me to pray for him.

And that Ye will save alive my father, and my
mother, and my brethren, and my sisters,
and all that they have, and deliver our lives
from death. Joshua 2:13

Two weeks later, I received another letter from Michael. His condition was deteriorating. His counselor was trying to get him a medical reprieve. This hurt me deeply. I felt trapped. There was nothing I could do to help him. I couldn't even see him. Grief weighed heavily upon me. God is the only person who has power over death. All we could do was pray. I cried out to God. It was a waiting game. What was going to happen next? It consumed all my thoughts. It left me unable to perform my daily work detail. For several days, I didn't go to work.

Four days after I got Mike's letter, I received a second letter. There was something else for me to worry about. It was from CJ. I thought it was a hoax. It had been almost a year since I had heard from her. When the letter arrived, I was glad to hear from her. This changed quickly when I read it. She accused me of something crazy. It wasn't the first time. Over the years, she insisted on numerous HIV tests. It just didn't make sense. What made her write me something so crazy? There were only two questions in the letter. She got my attention. It was as if she had been writing me all the time. This wasn't the case. This was the last thing I needed. It was another problem to deal with. The relationship was supposed to be over. I decide to call her. It was a pleasant telephone call. It gave me hope a reconciliation was possible.

To you, O LORD, I called; to the Lord I cried for mercy: Psalm 30:8 (NIV)

Shortly thereafter, I received another note from CJ. It said simply she might visit me on the coming Sunday. This made me feel good. Things were moving in the right direction. I had prayed for her. I had prayed for reconciliation. There was every reason to be hopeful.

Saturday night, I was reading a book. The officer in the control module called me. He informed me I needed to call home.

"Your sister said 'call home.'"

Two people came immediately to my mind, my mother and Mike. I started praying. What had happened? The call was made to my older brother. He informed me Mike had passed. My brother, Michael, died after we had both been locked up in the same prison. This hit me hard. The only good thing about it was we got a chance to spend more time together than we had in years. This was a pain I couldn't hold. It was what we had feared, one of us dying in prison. It was the one thing we said we didn't want to happen. Mike had died in prison. It hit close to home. It could have been me. My life could have ended behind bars. His death made me determined not to go back to prison. One of us had to break this cycle. Several people I knew had become seriously ill while they were in prison. I had watched them deteriorating. They were seriously ill away from home and their families. This was a fate I didn't want to suffer.

But in Your great mercy, You did not put an
end to them or abandon them, for You are a
gracious and merciful God.
Nehemiah 9:31 (NIV)

The next day, CJ came to see me. My sister Ann was with her. I was glad to see her. When I embraced CJ, it felt good. It helped to ease some of the pain. I had cried most of the night. Finally, I had taken something to help me sleep. We spoke very little during the visit. My mind was focussed on my grief.

It was obvious; our lives had taken another turn. We had reached another milestone in our relationship. Neither of us fully understood God's plan for our life was inconsistent with our own. We understood only somehow this was His Plan. He used Michael's death to help us put aside our differences.

Mr. and Mrs. Johnson

Shackles

This should be your ambition: to live a quiet life, minding your own business and working with your hands, just as we commanded you before.
1 Thessalonians 4:11 (NLT)

In recent years, I have had time to evaluate the cycles and shackles that almost ruined our lives. It has been more than two hundred years since *The Declaration of Independence* was signed. This event marked the end of slavery for African American people in the United States. Today, I see a new kind of slavery running rampant. There are still vestiges of the shackles that keep people trapped in bondage. At a recent book signing, a man made this comment to me.

"Your people sure have come a long way from the degradations of slavery. Look at you. Now, you are writing books."

Somehow, I believe he meant this as a compliment. After recovering from the shock of his words, I began to ponder them. They served as food for thought. I know very little about physical slavery. Sure, I have read books about slavery. I have watched movies about slavery. I have even heard stories about slavery. However, I know very little about the degradations of slavery to which he referred. I never experienced physical slavery.

There are other things I know about. There are other things I have experienced. As a result of these experiences, I ask these questions. How far have we really come from slavery? Is prejudice and injustice still prevalent? Is heaven going to be segregated? Does slavery still exist in a more discriminating form? Have we come far or are we on a slippery slope backward?

In looking around my environment, I'm disturbed by the answers. In many ways, our minds are still enslaved. What breaks my heart is we appear to enjoy it. In many cases, we resist change and growth. We remain more focussed on others than we do ourselves. There are not only vaguely transparent remnants of slavery and prejudice; there is also overt prejudice. It is not only prejudice between races; it's prejudice within the races. How do you break that shackle?

Families are at war with each other. Brothers are against brothers. Children are against parents. Nations are at war within the nation. There are wars and rumors of wars. The whole world appears to be in turmoil.

When I look at crime and the street game, we haven't come so far. The shackles of this cycle are very familiar to me. Friends still sell friends drugs. Friends still kill friends. Parents still introduce their children to the street games. Friends still disrespect each other. Women are still passed around like a party pack. Lives and families are still destroyed. Role models are still rare. People still remain trapped in the same cycles, year after year.

It has been said Sunday morning at 11:00 is the most segregated hour of the day. As I meet people with crosses, t-shirts, and religious paraphernalia saying they represent Christ, one thought runs through my mind.

"If it doesn't mean anything, just take it off."

This is because their attitude is not "Christ-like." When we say we are Christians, we are professing we represent Him. He's not rude. He's not arrogant. He's not trapped in traditions or ignorance. He doesn't choose His conversational tones based solely on race. How then are we supposed to integrate in heaven when we are segregated here? How will we ever break this shackle and learn to communicate as real brothers?

There is another form of enslavement I have watched. This one keeps our minds shackled. Our minds are fed sex, pornography, hatred, and immorality through books, movies, and television. Our children have lost their regard for life. Violence among youth is at an all time high. Many of them have lost respect for themselves and society. This is what they have learned from books, movies, and television.

We haven't come so far. In fact, it appears we have gone backwards! There is still hatred. There are deeper and more intense cycles. The shackles are tighter. They have disguised themselves. We have submitted willingly to their locks. By our unwillingness to be honest with ourselves, we have hindered our personal growth. We continue to destroy others to promote ourselves. Thus, we promote the cycles and the shackles.

But when He saw the multitudes, He was moved with compassion on them, because they fainted, and were scattered abroad, as sheep having no shepherd. Matthew 9:36

Am I saddened by all the shackles and cycles around me? No! I'm challenged. I'm inspired. I'm moved with compassion. Inside of me, there have to be answers. Surely, God has not shown me problems, which have no solutions. Hence, I ask myself these questions.

What can I do to ensure that not only my people, but brown people, white people, yellow people, and if need be green people have come a long way from the degradations of slavery? What can I do to make the world better? What can I do to break these cycles? What can I do to break these shackles? How can I help people to escape the vestiges of slavery?

> *Share each other's troubles and problems,*
> *and in this way obey the law of Christ.*
> Galatians 6:2 (NLT)

Perhaps, the answer is really simple. Maybe, the slaves had the answer years ago. It's in our ability to read. And what do we read? Are we to read only the things, which perpetrate the cycles in our lives? Are we only to read the books, which have no moral or redeeming value? If this is the choice, those who sacrificed their lives for the precious gift of reading died in vain. The cycles continue and the shackles remain. Thus, we remained trapped in the very degradations of slavery.

Epilogue

The Lord shall laugh at him: for He seeth that his day is coming. Psalm 37:13

Today, God has given me an amazing gift, the gift of laughter. I have always enjoyed laughing. At this time in my life, I don't need to use mood-altering drugs to achieve this euphoria. Laughing comes naturally in almost any circumstance. In some of the most painful situations of my life, I have found the gift of laughter. Some people have been offended by this gift. It's a gift they don't understand because they don't share its wealth.

I can imagine God sitting on His throne. He's roaring with laughter. He's laughing at the devil. The devil thought he had me. However, God, in His ultimate wisdom, was working all the time! He was working everything out for my good. In addition to this, He was working it out to help other people. Ultimately, He was working it out to ensure He gets the glory in my life. That's worth laughing about.

Special Acknowledgement

To all the nameless and faceless persons who were harmed directly or inadvertently by the cycles of corruption in our lives, we sincerely apologize and beg your forgiveness.

This is the message He has given us to announce to you: God is light and there is no darkness in Him at all.

1 JOHN 1:5 (NLT)

NOTES